AUDIT COMMITTEES IN LARGE UK COMPANIES

by

Paul Collier
University of Exeter

This report has been prepared for the Research Board of the ICAEW. The views expressed are those of the authors and are not necessarily shared by the Research Board or the Council of the Institute.

No responsibility for loss occasioned to any person acting or refraining from action as a result of any material in this publication can be accepted by the authors or publishers.

Published by
The Research Board
The Institute of Chartered Accountants in England and Wales,
Chartered Accountants' Hall,
P.O. Box 433,
Moorgate Place,
London, EC2P 2BJ.

Contents

Acknowledgements

The author wishes to record his appreciation to the Auditing Research Foundation of The Institute of Chartered Accountants in England and Wales and the Bank of England for their funding and support of the project on which the report is based.

Thanks is also given to the finance directors and other officers of the industrial concerns and financial institutions, who completed the questionnaire and in some cases discussed various aspects of the research with me. Finally, thanks is due to the partners of major professional firms, who assisted with information gathering and were prepared to be interviewed. Obviously, without their input the research would not have been possible.

Executive Summary

The book reports the results of a questionnaire survey of the Times top 250 industrial companies and 50 major financial institutions undertaken in January 1991. The findings discussed in this summary are based upon the responses of over 80% of those surveyed.

The number of organisations with an AC

Overall 53% of industrial companies and 88% of financial institutions had an AC. The incidence of ACs varied according to the type of organisation. Virtually all public sector industrial companies and privatised industrial companies had an AC. Two–thirds of UK listed industrial companies had an AC. ACs were infrequent in industrial companies which were unquoted or subsidiaries of foreign companies. ACs were present in almost 90% of the financial institutions. The only exception was subsidiaries of foreign banks as only 44% of these had an AC.

Although some companies have had an AC for over 20 years, the widespread adoption of ACs appears to have been a relatively recent phenomenon as over half of the ACs surveyed had been established in the five years preceding the survey.

The motives for having an AC

The main motive reported by companies for having an AC was a desire to follow good corporate practice. Other important motives for respondents were: to assist the directors in discharging their statutory responsibilities as regards financial reporting; strengthening the role and effectiveness of non-executive directors; and enhancing the independence of internal and external auditors.

AC practices and procedures

The practices and procedures of ACs in industrial companies and financial institutions were broadly similar.

The majority of ACs were composed solely of non-executive directors. The number of committee members varied from two to eleven but the typical AC had three or four non-executive members who were appointed by the board or were automatically members by virtue of being non-executive directors. Appointments were normally for an indefinite term.

The ACs generally met between two and four times per year. The typical meeting lasted around two hours and the total average annual meeting time was approximately seven hours. The duties and responsibilities of ACs are usually laid down in board minutes, terms of reference or both. Minutes are produced for all AC meetings. The AC minutes are widely distributed and are certainly received by the AC and the board.

Functions assigned to ACs

A wide range of functions were assigned to ACs by the respondents. The breadth of functions assigned to the ACs is demonstrated by the number reported as being present in over 70% of respondents with an AC. The functions were:

External reporting

Review company accounting principles and practice, and significant changes during the year

Review audited annual financial statements

Review interim reports

External auditors

Discuss with the auditors their experiences and problems in carrying out the audit

Discuss the meaning and significance of audited figures and notes attached thereto

Review their evaluation of the company's internal control systems, recommendations to management and management's response

Review factors that might impair, or be perceived to impair the auditor's independence

Internal auditors

Discuss the effectiveness of internal controls

Review internal audit objectives and plans

Discuss with the internal auditors their findings and reports

Ascertain whether proper action has been taken on recommendations

Evaluate the adequacy of the resources devoted to internal audit

Review organisation of the department, lines and reporting and independence of the internal audit function

Discuss with the auditors their experiences and problems in carrying out the audit

Discuss the relationship between internal and external auditors and the co-ordination of their audit work

Factors affecting the effectiveness of ACs

The respondents agreed that the most important attributes of AC members for a successful AC were personal qualities, like sound judgement and independence from management, and a full understanding of the purposes and responsibilities of the AC.

The most important factors that contributed to the success of ACs were identified by respondents as the availability of relevant information, like provision of an agenda and related material in advance of meetings, and ready access to external auditors and internal auditors.

Disclosure of information about ACs

Approximately 70% of respondents disclosed some information about their AC in the annual report and accounts. The commonest form of disclosure, adopted by almost three quarters of respondents disclosing information on their AC, was to detail the existence of the AC and the identity of AC members. An extension of disclosure to include the objectives and functions of the AC was provided by only 12 companies.

Chapter 1

Introduction

Objectives

This paper, sponsored by the Auditing Research Foundation of The Institute of Chartered Accountants in England and Wales in conjunction with the Bank of England, presents the results of a questionnaire survey of audit committees in major industrial and financial entities in the UK. The research instrument and subsequent follow up work had the following objectives:

    (i)   identify the major UK industrial and financial entities, that have an audit committee (AC) as at January 1991;

    (ii)   gather basic data on AC practices and procedures, the functions assigned to ACs and the factors seen as affecting the effectiveness of ACs;

    (iii)   investigate the reasons why some companies choose not to have an AC;

    (iv)   attempt to identify factors which might explain why some companies have an AC and others do not; and

    (v)   examine the extent of information about ACs disclosed in the accounts.

1

Definition

ACs are defined by reference to their composition and function. Examples of definitions from a professional body, a professional firm and a research survey in chronological order include:

> the definition chosen by the Accountants International Study Group (1977), which was taken from CICA (1976).
> A committee of directors of a corporation whose specific responsibility is to review the annual financial statements before submission to the board of directors. The committee generally acts as liaison between the auditor and the board of directors and its activities may include the review of nomination of the auditors, overall scope of the audit, results of the audit, internal financial controls and financial information for publication.

Peat Marwick McLintock (1987).

> An AC is a committee of the board of directors established to give additional assurance regarding the quality and reliability of financial information used by the board. An audit committee of a company may be broadly defined as a committee of the board, composed wholly or predominantly of non-executive directors, set up to oversee, review and monitor the financial reporting process and the audit activities.

Marrian (1988)

A committee of the board normally comprising three to five directors with no operating responsibility in financial management. Its primary tasks are to review the financial statements, the effectiveness of the company's accounting and internal control systems, and the findings of the auditors, and to make recommendations on the appointment and remuneration of the external auditors.

The definitions agree that an AC is a committee of directors concerned with audit, internal control systems and financial reporting. The membership in the latter two definitions emphasises non-executive director participation. ACs should consist solely of non-executive directors or non-executive directors should be in the majority. For the purposes of the research, ACs were widely defined. ACs must have at least one non-executive director and have some involvement with auditing. The reason for not requiring a majority of non-executive directors is that in some companies there is confusion between being 'in attendance' and 'membership'. For example, in some companies the finance director is a member of the AC while in others the finance director, although present at all meetings, is not a member. The compromise of one non-executive director emphasises the independent director input and ensures that the research covers the full range of AC practice.

The debate

ACs are not a new concept and a number of firms have had ACs for a long period. In the US discussion of the usefulness of ACs has a 50 year history (Birkett 1986) but in the UK the overwhelming majority of ACs have come into existence since 1970 (Marrian 1988). Nor can ACs be viewed in isolation; rather they are part of a wider discussion on corporate governance. Recent developments in corporate governance have focused on the role and duties of non-executive directors. There has been a trend towards companies appointing non-executive directors (Bank of England 1985, 1988). The latest Bank of England survey of the Times 1000 shows that only 11% of respondents had no non-executive directors while in 60% of cases the board included three or more such directors and in 60% of cases the non-executive directors constituted over 30% of the board. Pressure still continues and recent significant pronouncements about the desirability of non-executive directors include:

3

Revised code on non-executive directors from **PRO NED** (1987). The code stated that in quoted companies boards are more likely to be effective if they have strong, independent non-executive directors. In large quoted companies it is recommended that the board should have at least three independent non-executive directors. The main tasks of non-executive directors are: to contribute an independent view to the board's deliberations; to help the board provide the company with effective leadership; to ensure the continuing effectiveness of the executive directors and management and to ensure high standards of financial probity in the company.

In 1990 the Institute of Directors (IOD) called for the compulsory appointment of non-executives to company boards and stated that the IOD would support investor pressure for legal or regulatory provisions for the appointment non-executives.[1]

The Association of British Insurers (1991) also stressed that as a matter of good practice 'non-executive directors should be sufficient in number and calibre for their views to carry significant weight on the board'. The Institutional Shareholders' Committee (ISC) (1991) took a similar line in a statement of best practice. The ISC recommended that non-executive directors should be independent and suggested independence was assured when the director had not been: employed in an executive capacity by the company within the last few years; is not retained

---

[1] Financial Times, 'IOD Backs Pressure for Non-Executive Board Appointments', 23 November 1990, p. 7.

as a professional advisor; and is not a significant supplier or customer of the company.[2]

The Institute of Chartered Accountants in England and Wales (ICAEW) (1991) study group on the changing role of the non-executive director recommended that:
All listed companies should appoint independent non-executive directors as should major private companies;

Non-executive directors should comprise around a third of the board and ideally there should be at least three non-executive directors; and

A code of practice for non-executive directors should be prepared.

Parallel to this development have been calls for companies to set up ACs. Partly because ACs are a means of involving and empowering non-executive directors and partly in response to the need for improved audit, financial control and financial reporting. The calls come from the same and other sources including:

The Companies (Audit Committees) Bill 1988, which aimed to give shareholders the power to insist on the appointment of ACs and non-executive directors. The bill was defeated in the Lords after successfully completing the committee stage. The defeat was attributable to a reluctance to legislate in this area rather than an antipathy towards the concept of ACs. The Labour Party during the Committee stages of the Companies Act 1989 also proposed

---

[2] Bank of England (1985) found that a third of non-executive directors were former executives or had professional connections. Bank of England (1988) reported that at least 75% of non-executive directors fell outside this category.

setting up ACs for all public limited companies but were vetoed by the government. More recently Shadow Corporate Affairs Minister Ms Majorie Mowlam has hinted at the possibility of legislation to set up ACs[3] and Austin Mitchell MP (1991) in an address to the Chartered Association of Certified Accountants not only recommended ACs but also stated 'I am interested in changing the corporate power structure with appropriate checks and balances built in. I want to see audit committees include representatives of consumers, employees, shareholders, pensioners and other interests' – a move towards the AC being a supervisory board in a two-tier structure.

Encouragement from various bodies, such as the IOD, PRO NED, the Stock Exchange and the Bank of England, for the formation of ACs in public companies. Examples include: the IOD called for legislation or regulation to require listed companies to have an AC; the revised PRO NED code (1987) had similar provisions to assist non-executive directors in carrying out their tasks; and the ICAEW (1991) contained a recommendation on ACs and set out details of their composition and functions.

The ICAEW (1987) submission to the Department of Trade and Industry on the Eighth Directive supported a statutory role for ACs in all public companies as a means of maintaining and protecting the independence of auditors.

International developments in North American with the publication of the Treadway Commission (National Commission on Fraudulent Financial Reporting 1987) in the US and the Mac-

---

[3] Accountancy Age, Analysis, 25.4.1991, p. 13 and Accountancy Age, 'Fraud reporting duty called for by Labour', 29.8.1991, p. 2. In the latter, Ms M. Mowlam was reported as calling for 'audit committees with the active participation of non-executive directors' to be made compulsory'.

Donald Commission (Commission to Study the Public's Expectations of Audits 1988) in Canada. Both recommended an expansion of the role of Audit Committees and have been linked to the UK debate.

This project will provide a means of measuring the development of ACs since the Marrian (1988) survey and assessing the influence of the continuing corporate governance debate.

Benefits from ACs

ACs involve the interaction between the company and the wider world in terms of shareholders and external auditors. AC members are usually directors and as directors are elected by the shareholders, the AC is representative of the shareholders. The AC also is an important point of contact between the external auditors and the board. Internally the AC interfaces with the internal auditors and management. Thus, the AC links the internal organisation represented by management and internal auditors with the external world of shareholders and external auditors. Kalbers (1989) points out that in the US recommendations, rules and laws set requirements and expectations for the AC. This framework links the company with standard setters, self-regulatory bodies and regulatory agencies. Current literature on ACs from professional firms (see for example Coopers & Lybrand Deloitte 1990 or Peat Marwick McLintock 1987) and professional bodies (see for example AISG 1977, CICA 1981 and Marrian 1988) present the argument for ACs by identifying the following benefits to the parties involved:

Directors

Help directors meet their statutory (Companies Acts 1985, 1989 and Insolvency Act 1986) and fiduciary responsibilities, especially as regards accounting records, annual accounts and the audit.

Improve communication between the board and the external auditors. The AC will meet the external auditors on several occasions during the year and be able to investigate the annual accounts, audit and quality of internal controls more thoroughly than would be possible if the review of these matters were left to the full board, which might only see the auditors once a year. The AC also acts as a filter that ensures that the board only considers the most important items relating to audit, accounting and internal control.

Strengthen the role of the independent non-executive director by formalising their work in a key business area.

Aid non-executive directors in their knowledge and understanding of: the business; financial statements; accounting and control systems; and the nature and scope of statutory audit and internal audit.

Enable non-executive directors to bring their wider business knowledge to bear on accounting, auditing and internal control difficulties.

External auditors

Enhance the external auditor's independent position as the external auditor can communicate directly with those directors who are not actively engaged in the management of the firm. A view supported by a Canadian study (CICA, 1981) which reported that 72% of external auditors indicated that the existence of an AC 'enhanced their perceived independence, making it easier for them to be objective and not to be subject to undue influence by management'. However as Wolnizer (1987) comments, the capacity of ACs to enhance external auditor independence and provide an independent review is limited by the education, experience and independence of the members of the AC.

Improve communications between the external auditors and the directors. The AC causes the external auditors and a subset of directors to meet on a normal and regular basis and overcomes the difficulties identified by Mautz and Neuman (1970) who reported that in firms without an AC there was little communication between the board and external auditors because external auditors were reluctant to go over the heads of operating management to the board.

Pressure management into acting on recommendations made.

Internal auditors

Raise the status of the internal audit function by giving internal auditors access to board members. This line of communication should encourage internal auditors to enhance the quality of their work and raise their esteem among managers who will be aware that internal auditors have this line of communication.

Enhance the independence of internal auditors. The Treadway Commission (1987) discouraged the situation where the internal audit function reports to the senior officer directly responsible for preparing the accounts. Instead it suggests that internal auditors report to the chief executive officer and in many companies there is a dual reporting responsibility to the chief executive and the AC (see for example Williams 1988 describing the position at Warner-Lambert Company). Miller (1988) opines that 'The best liability insurance coverage a corporate board can have is an effective internal audit department' and argues that the AC is crucial in determining the effectiveness of the internal audit department as it ensures the independence of the function and reviews the scope, results and quality of its' work.

Improves communication between the board and the internal audit function. Prior to ACs it was rare for internal auditors to report to more than one board member and certainly to a director without management responsibilities. The AC provides a forum in which a subset of directors can consider internal audit work and scope and filter matters for consideration by the main board.

Pressure management into acting on recommendations made.

Shareholders and the public

Increase the credibility and objectivity of financial reports by demonstrating the board's intention to give due weight to reviewing external reporting, auditing, internal controls and other related matters. This argument presupposes that shareholders understand the relevance of an AC and that the company discloses the existence of the AC (Marrian 1988 showed that around half the respondents with ACs did not disclose their existence in their accounts).

Dangers with ACs

The formation of ACs in companies presents certain dangers. A review of a similar literature to that covered for benefits, reveals the following concerns:

Encroachment on the functions of the executive and dilution of executive authority. An AC must have well-defined objectives, possibly in a charter or written terms of reference to prevent the AC, when conducting an independent review, from straying outside its' audit, accounting and internal control brief.

ACs can have a divisive effect because during meetings there can be criticism of management on accounting, internal control and financial reporting matters without those discussed being present to put their viewpoint or having the right of timely reply.

The diversion of non-executive directors from their main role of providing a wider view during the determination of corporate strategy and other board deliberations into the routine matters of audit and financial reporting.

ACs are a step towards radical changes in corporate governance and possibly a first step towards two-tier boards, as initially envisaged in the draft EEC fifth directive. The AC constituted with a wider membership, perhaps including employees representatives and others, could undertake a supervisory role.

ACs might reduce contact between the auditors and main board and may mean that many executive directors will have no contact with the auditors. The delegation of the functions typically assigned to ACs may cause unease on the main board if the AC is largely composed of non-executive directors who are not

11

directly involved in management and may not fully appreciate the complexity of auditing and accounting matters under discussion.

ACs are only as good as the non-executive directors on them and for an effective AC the membership must combine a good knowledge of the business with a technical understanding of internal controls, disclosure practices and auditing. There are also concerns that ACs are ineffective because inadequate time is given to their meetings or they do not have the relevant technical expertise available to advise them.

Structure of the report

The report has seven further chapters. Chapter 2 examines the development of ACs in the UK, US, Canada, Australia and New Zealand and identifies the major events. Chapter 3 reviews previous research into ACs and the current state of information about ACs. The majority of research was undertaken in the US. The results provide only a limited insight into AC effectiveness and why some companies voluntarily have ACs and others do not. Chapter 4 comprises the research methodology, the compilation of the questionnaire, populations to be covered, response rates and the effect of non-response bias. Chapters 5 and 6 describe the results of the questionnaire. Chapter 7 companies the results from the two populations surveyed and Chapter 8 discusses the conclusions to be drawn from the research and the opportunities for further research in the area.

Summary

The research aims to provide a definitive picture of the spread of ACs in major UK firms. The research also hopes to provide information on typical AC practices and procedures, the functions assigned to ACs and the factors that contribute to effective ACs. The information gathered should also lead to the formation of testable hypotheses.

Chapter 2

The Development of Audit Committees

Introduction

ACs are found in the companies of a number of countries. This chapter reviews the developments towards ACs in the UK and elsewhere.

United Kingdom

ACs are not new. Tricker (1978) quoted a 'Report of the Audit Committee' of the Great Western Railway dated 1872. This relates to a period when auditors were drawn from the shareholders of the company, with professional accountants employed to assist them. In the first half of the 20th century it was common practice for auditors to attend board meetings and to be seen to be acting independently of management. More recently the independence of auditors has been questioned. It has been argued that although shareholders are legally responsible for appointing the auditor and fixing his remuneration in practice they are merely following board recommendations. As boards typically have a majority of executive directors and the auditor works closely with management, this reduces the independence of the auditor from management. In the 1970s ACs were proposed as a possible solution to this problem by a number of sources including:

the major accounting firms, who throughout the 1970s produced booklets[4] recommending ACs;

the professional journals, for example in 1976 the editorial in the 1000th issue of Accountancy was a call for the formation of ACs in major companies;

the government in a White Paper (1977)[5] on the conduct of directors;

The CBI working party in 1977 stated that 'The operation of audit committees within certain companies might be an effective method of ensuring the independent review of those companies' financial activities, of improving the existing internal and external audit procedures and of letting it be seen that the requirements were met'.

Accountancy bodies through the Consultative Committee of Accountancy Bodies Audit Practices Committee, (CCAB, 1977) which stated that 'experimentation with audit committees by companies should be encouraged'.

The Accountants International Study Group (1977) and the examples of the US and Canada;

---

[4] For example: Arthur Andersen & Co. (1972), 'The Audit Committee and the Board of Directors'; Price Waterhouse & Co. (1973), 'The Audit Committee'; Coopers & Lybrand, (1974), 'An Audit Committee'; Peat Marwick Mitchell & Co. (1976), 'The Audit Committee'; and Touche Ross & Co. (1977), 'The Audit Committee - A Look at the Development of Audit Committees in Canada, the USA and the UK'.

[5] White Paper, Cmnd. 7037. 'The Conduct of Company Directors', Presented to Parliament, November 1977.

Leading industrialists – 1979 Peter Macadam, the chairman of BAT Industries at the 1979 Annual Conference of the Institute of Chartered Accountants[6] extolled the virtues of an AC as a means of ensuring that the supervisory task with respect to control is undertaken successfully; and

practitioners like: Charlton (1976); Byrd (1977); or Jubb (1979).

There were also attempts at introducing legislation on ACs under the auspices of Sir Brandon Rhys Williams, who since 1970 annually introduced a debate calling for audit committees. In 1975-76, the Companies (Audit Committees) Bill was introduced but it was defeated on the second reading in 1976-77.[7] The Bill aimed to amend the law with respect to the appointment and functions of non-executive directors, auditors and ACs in major public companies. The Bill required companies to set up ACs with at least three non-executive directors. The function of the AC was to review all audited or unaudited financial statements prior to their submission to the board and to report thereon to the board.

The pressure continued throughout the 1980s and into the 1990s. Significant events and sources of pressure during this period include:

PRO NED (Promotion of Non-Executive Directors) - formed in 1982. Sponsors included The Bank of England; The Committee of London Clearing Banks; The Committee of Scottish Clearing Banks; The Institutional Shareholders Committee; The Stock Exchange; and The Confederation of British Industry. PRO

---

6 Macadam, P. (1979), 'Reporting Responsibility of the Board - the Auditor and the Audit Committee', BAT Industries, Group Public Affairs Department.

7 Companies (Audit Committees) Bill, 1975-76, 247, ii, 131. Companies (Audit Committees) Bill, 1976-77, 49, i, 589.

NED issued a new code of recommended practice in April 1987. The code (Promotion of Non-Executive Directors' 1987) recommended that non-executive directors should be consulted on major issues of audit and control - tasks that will be facilitated by the formation of an AC. The functions of the AC should be to consider and make recommendations to the board about important financial information, the adequacy of systems of financial control, the scope of the audit and auditors' remuneration. The AC should be composed mainly of non-executive directors and its chairpersonship and quorum should reflect this.

ICAEW - in 1986 an ICAEW working party on the future of the audit recognised that ACs could have responsibilities in respect of the appointment and remuneration of auditors, the review and approval of audit plans and the review of management reports issued by auditors. The working party reported that for ACs to be effective they must be independent. Further, in February 1987 The Institute of Chartered Accountants in England and Wales (1987) in response to Eighth Company Law Directive stated 'We can see arguments to support a statutory requirement for an audit committee in all public companies and in all companies where there is a substantial public interest'.

EC Directives - the draft Fifth Directive on the structure of company boards and the Eighth Directive on the independence and integrity of auditors have lead to debates about ACs and corporate governance and the role of ACs in strengthening auditor independence. In particular, the draft Fifth Directive requires a majority of non-executive directors on the board and such an environment may well be linked to further AC formation.

Bank of England - in January 1987 the Bank of England issued a consultative paper that encouraged the formation of ACs in banks.

17

The Stock Exchange - in 1987 the chairman of the Stock Exchange wrote to all listed and USM companies recommending that they followed the PRO NED code. In the same year, the Stock Exchange introduced a requirement in the 'Continuing Obligations' section of the Yellow Book for companies to identify non-executive directors in the annual accounts, together with brief biographical details.

The House of Commons - the Companies Bill (Audit Committees) 1988[8] attempted to legislate in favour of non-executive directors and ACs in public companies with the objective of forming an independent counterbalance to the executive of the company.

The Bill had three main proposals;

the directors report of public companies should indicate the directors who are independent directors;

if the number of independent directors on the board of a major public company[9] is below three, the annual report should indicate whether additional appointments are proposed;

the shareholders of a major public company should have the right to vote to require a major public company without an AC to form one.

---

[8] Companies (Audit Committees) Bill, 1986-87, 69, 10:02:87; Companies (Audit Committees) Bill, 1986-87, 162, 13:05:87; Companies (Audit Committees) Bill, 1987-88, 130. 22:03:88.; Companies (Audit Committees) Bill, 1987-88, House of Lords, Vol. 1, 73.

[9] Meeting two out of the following three conditions - annual turnover greater than £200 million, assets of over £100 million and more than 2000 full-time employees.

The AC specified by the Bill was to be governed by model regulations with the following provisions:

not less than three independent directors;

at least two meetings per year;

auditors to be notified of meetings and have the right to request a meeting;

AC meetings should be minuted and the minutes circulated to directors;

functions of the AC are to review financial statements prior to publication; meet the auditors; and make recommendations on the appointment and remuneration of auditors; and

report via the annual financial statement whether the board has properly considered its reports.

The Institutional Shareholders Committee (1991) argued for sufficient non-executive directors both in number and calibre and referred to 'a growing awareness of the value of audit committees'.

1991 The study group of the ICAEW on the changing role of the non-executive directors recommended:

4.10 All listed companies should appoint an audit committee. The study group also recommends that all private companies should also follow this practice.

4.11 The directors' report included with the annual financial statements of listed companies should state whether or not an audit committee of the board exists.

4.12 If a company does not have a formal audit committee, the non-executive directors should meet the company's external auditors at least once a year.

The study group also opine that, provided there is an effective non-executive director presence on the board and an AC with a majority of non-executive directors, the Fifth Directive proposal that a single tier board should have a majority of non-executive members is unnecessary.

International comparison - the examples of Canada and the US, where ACs are accepted practice and are perceived as being effective, have been cited as reasons for UK companies to set up ACs.

Canada

The collapse of the Atlantic Acceptance Corporation Limited in 1965 led to a reappraisal of financial practices and corporate governance. The Royal Commission report on the collapse (Hughes 1969) recommended that 'an audit committee, consisting of not less than three directors of a company, the majority of whom should not be officers[10] or otherwise employed by the company, should review the company's financial statements before approval by the board of directors, and should confer with the auditors'. In Ontario the Lawrence Commit-

---

[10] Officers include officer directors (executive directors) and other employees.

tee[11] recommended that ACs should be required by companies issuing equity shares. The recommendation was supported by a CICA committee on shareholders' audits[12] and Ontario enacted a requirement for ACs in The Business Corporations Act 1970. This lead was followed by the British Columbia (Company Act 1973) and Federal legislation under the Canada Business Corporations Act 1975. This legislation, plus subsequent Acts in Manitoba and Saskatchewan, require corporations offering securities to the public to have an AC of not fewer than three directors. The majority of the members on the committee must not be officers or employees of the corporation or its affiliates. The statutory responsibilities of the AC are to review the financial statements prior to approval by the board. The auditor, who is entitled to receive notices of all meetings of the AC, may be required by the AC to attend meetings and has a right to appear before and be heard by the committee at any meeting.

The McDonald Commission, CICA (1988), reviewing the success of this statutory approach saw much merit in audit committees but believed that the ultimate safeguard of auditing standards was a dedication to professionalism from the auditors.

Singapore

The only other country to have a statutory requirement to form ACs is Singapore. Singapore, influenced by the US and Canada examples and as a means of reinforcing the financial credibility of the companies on the stock exchange, in the Companies Act 1989 requires every

---

[11] Ontario Legislative Assembly, (1967), Interim Report of the Select Committee on Company Law, p. 82.

[12] Report of Special Committee Shareholders' Audits, (1968) CA magazine, November, pp. 6-10.

company admitted to the official list of the Singapore Stock Exchange to have an AC. The AC must be composed of at least three directors of whom the majority must neither be an executive director of the company or related corporations nor a close relation of any executive director of the company or related corporation. Section (21/5) states that the functions of the AC are to:

> review with the auditor: the audit plan; his evaluation of the system of internal accounting controls; his audit report; and assistance given by the company.

> review the scope and results of internal audit procedures.

> review the financial statements and submit them to the board.

> nominate the auditor.

The auditor has the right to appear and be heard at any meeting of the AC and can require the AC to meet to consider matters that the auditor believes should be brought to the attention of the AC. The AC may require the auditor to appear before them.

United States

ACs have a long history in the US. In 1940 the SEC recommended in the aftermath of the McKesson and Robbins Inc. fraud that a committee of independent directors should nominate the auditors and arrange the details of the engagement (Accounting Series Release No. 19). In 1972 the recommendation was endorsed for all publicly owned by Accounting Series Release No. 123 and in 1974 Accounting Series Release No. 165 introduced a requirement for publicly owned companies to disclose the existence and composition of ACs. In 1977 the NYSE adopted a ruling that all corporations listed should have an

AC. The ruling became effective on 30 June 1978. The AC was to be comprised solely of directors independent of management and free from any relationship that might impair the exercise of independent judgement. More recently the national Association of Security Dealers (1987) brought in a similar requirement.

The Treadway Commission (1987) in their final report recommended that all publicly owned companies be required to have ACs consisting solely of independent directors. The report also made a series of recommendations on the running of ACs. The proposals included:

a written charter for the AC specifying duties and responsibilities;

ACs should have adequate resources and authority to initiate investigations, including the right to seek the opinion of legal or outside experts;

disclosure in the annual report of the responsibilities, activities and membership of the AC;

responsibility for: overseeing the financial reporting process; the independence of the external auditor; the review of internal audit role, functions, work and independence; and the review of compliance with the company's code of conduct.

New membership requirements for CPA Firms SEC Practice Section were introduced in 1986. The terms dealt with six items for auditors to communicate to ACs. The items are material errors, irregularities or illegal acts; material weaknesses in internal control; opinions management obtain from independent accountants; accounting disclosure considerations re material contingencies; significant accounting disclosure decisions; and changes in accounting principle. The disclosures supplement the existing rules, which covered the disclosure of significant accounting, auditing and reporting disagreements with management; and the fees received in the year for management advisory services. The requirement for auditors to communicate with ACs was strengthened in 1988 by the issue of Statement on Auditing Standards (SAS) No. 61 dealing with communications with ACs. The standard was applicable to all entities with an AC or equivalent and SEC engagements. The matters for communication include: the nature of the auditor's responsibility; significant accounting policies; the process used by management to make accounting estimates; significant audit adjustments; disagreements with management; major issues discussed with management; and difficulties encountered in performing the audit. Mention of ACs is also made in SAS No. 53 (The Auditor's Responsibility to Detect and Report Errors and Irregularities), SAS No. 54 (Illegal Acts by Clients) and SAS No. 60 (Communication of Internal Control Structure Related Matters Notes in an Audit). The US has managed without legislation to force major companies to have ACs and has introduced standards for communications between the auditors and ACs.

Australia and New Zealand

In Australia and New Zealand there has been no statutory legislation to require the formation of ACs nor are there any stock exchange requirements for ACs. In Australia, the Corporate Affairs Commission (1979) endorsed, after an enquiry into the affairs of Gollin Holdings, the principle that companies should be encouraged to have ACs. However, there has been no pressure for the formation of ACs from the government, the professional accountancy bodies (beyond a discussion document issued by the Australian Society of Accountants 1980) or the Australian Associated Stock Exchanges. Although there have been no recent surveys the consensus is that few Australian companies have an AC.[13] In New Zealand, according to Bradbury (1979, 1990) there has been a minimal interest in ACs. Explanations cited for this are that audit committees and corporate governance have not become a political issues and that New Zealand is a low-litigation environment.

Continental Europe

Tricker (1978) stated 'They do not have audit committees elsewhere in Europe: perhaps because they are not necessary with alternative forms of corporate governance'. The position appears to have changed little, as Van Hoek (1988) stated that 'audit committees are little known in Europe' citing the responses to a question in a survey performed by IFAC in 1985 within the framework of the European Confederation of Institutes of Internal Audit; and European Economic Community directives are silent on ACs.

Summary

ACs in the form discussed in this paper are confined to countries with anglo-saxon systems of corporate governance. Although ACs are not new they have been promoted as possible solutions to: problems arising from financial scandals; defining a role for non-executive directors; external auditor independence; and other difficulties. The uptake of the concept of ACs is widespread in the US and Canada, where ACs are virtually mandatory for major companies, but elsewhere, although there is some growth, the picture is less clear.

---

[13] 'Several Australian public companies have voluntarily established audit committees, and it is expected that more will do so in the future.' Pound, G.D., Willingham, J.J. and Carmichael, D.R. (1986), 'Australian Auditing: Concepts and Methods', McGraw-Hill, Sydney.

Chapter 3

A Review of Previous Research into Audit Committees

Introduction

Research into ACs falls into three categories:

(i)   surveys of the extent to which companies have an AC, the composition, practices and procedures of ACs, and opinions on ACs and matters related thereto;

(ii)   studies testing hypotheses on the effectiveness of ACs; and

(iii)   studies attempting to explain why some companies have ACs and others do not.

Survey research

Survey research has been carried out in the United Kingdom, United States of America and Canada.

United Kingdom

The first survey into ACs in the UK was carried out by Tricker (1978). The project, which was targeted at the independent director and the AC, involved case study work at 15 companies. Two of the companies (13%) had an AC, three companies (20%) intended to form one in the foreseeable future, two companies that had not considered the possibility of having an AC and the remaining eight did not intend to form an AC. Tricker commented that the value of ACs was not widely appreciated and observed that the lead in the creation of ACs was being taken by the clearing banks, a few large companies and some pioneering small companies.

Chambers and Snook (1979), undertook questionnaire research on ACs. The population identified for sampling was the top 250 companies the Times list and 73 organisations at the top of the Times lists of financial concerns. Responses were received from approximately three-quarters of each group. The existence of an AC was reported by 11% of financial institutions and 13% of industrial concerns. Even after allowing for plans to create ACs in the two years after the survey, 80% of the top UK industrial and financial entities did not have or intend to form an AC. Other findings included:

> ACs were a relatively recent feature as 90% of the 31 ACs had been formed since 1975. The researchers reported that the rate of formation appeared to be accelerating (although Marrian 1988 subsequently showed that 1978 was the peak year for AC formation).

> Numerous reasons were put forward for creating an AC but only the roles of ACs as a means of delegation/specialisation to make the board more efficient and as a forum for dialogue and liaison between the board and external auditors were mentioned by over six (19%) of respondents with ACs.

> The main responsibilities of ACs related to the audit process. Among the responsibilities mentioned most frequently were: air the criticisms and recommendations of the auditors and check the appropriate action is taken; examine and review with the auditors the scope and the results of their audit; and review the external audit programme. Half of the respondents included external reporting functions in the remit of the AC. The functions

27

mentioned included: oversee the production of the annual report and accounts; review the annual and interim financial statements; discuss accounting principles, policies and practices; and review accounting policy changes and the effects of changes in accounting standards. A similar prominence was given by the firms to systems and control matters like a review of the internal control system and the adequacy of financial controls and internal checks. Only a third of respondents indicated that there was active consideration of internal audit matters such as the scope and results of internal audit work and the functions and activities of the internal audit department. About a quarter of ACs had responsibilities for finance and expenditure matters. The functions covered included: a review of the financial position of the group; and to consider and note proposals on various financial targets and capital expenditure. It was suggested that these functions may be a legacy from finance committees that had evolved into ACs. The duties of the AC were formally specified in 87% of the cases and were generally ratified by the board.

The typical AC comprised three non-executive and one executive member. The research reported that older ACs had less non-executive directors and more executive members than ACs established more recently. The average number of members was 3.4 and the AC typically met three times per year for two to three hours. One meeting to coincide with the interim and annual reports respectively plus one other meeting.

In late 1985 Marrian (1988) sent a short questionnaire about ACs to the Times Top 1000 industrial companies; 451 replies were received and 17% of respondents indicated that they had an AC. Subsequently interviews with respondents were carried out at 59 companies. The interviews showed that:

28

ACs were a relatively new phenomenon. All the ACs had been set up since 1970 and all but four of the 59 ACs reviewed were established after 1975. The peek year was 1978[14] when 12 ACs were formed but the rate of expansion has continued into the 1980s with 32% of the ACs being set up in the period 1982-1985. Although, the researcher was 'unable to get a clear picture of whether or not respondents felt that ACs were growing in number'; there was some evidence that the number of companies establishing ACs is growing;

the formation of ACs is often the result of pressure from one person or a small group in the company based on their experience of ACs elsewhere;

ACs typically were composed of four non-executive directors and met twice a year. Meetings were conducted formally with an agenda, minutes and formal reports from the internal and external auditors. The deliberations of the AC were reported formally to the board.

The terms of reference of ACs varied greatly but usually comprised, as shown in Table 1, dealings with internal and external auditors, the financial statements and internal control.

United States of America

In the US, Mautz and Neuman (1970, 1977) carried out the first major studies of ACs. Both surveys targeted four groups: corporate

---

[14] Marrian (1988) suggests that the peak is possibly a reaction to the intimation to government by the Consultative Committee of Accountancy Bodies Audit Practice Committee in 1977 that 'experimentation with audit committees by companies should be encouraged'.

management; non-officer directors; independent auditors; and internal auditors.

Table 1

Remit of ACs found in over 10% of the sample examined by Marrian (1988)

Function of the AC	% of sample
Relationships with external auditors	90
Review statutory accounts and other published financial information	70
The operation of the internal audit department	51
Examination of the accounting and internal control systems	47
Arrangements for compliance with statutory reporting requirements	38
Review sensitive payments or activities that may be harmful to the companies reputation	19

Few ACs became involved in setting the fees of the auditors; and 93% of the companies viewed ACs as being worthwhile.

The 1970 study examined the extent of AC use, operating practices, purposes and functions, and opinions on the effectiveness of ACs. Approximately 32% of the companies responding had ACs. The results showed that ACs were not a new phenomenon as some 30% of the companies had an AC that was over 20 years old; nevertheless there was a recent expansion of interest in ACs as 40% of the ACs had been formed since 1965. The research revealed a varied picture as regards the composition, functions and success of the ACs covered. In general ACs were small (two to four members), had a majority of non-executive members, but few were limited to non-executive directors, and meet twice a year for one to two hours. The minimum functions assigned to ACs were to meet with the auditors and discuss the audit and the financial report. However there were wide differences in the involvement of the AC with internal control, internal audit and other matters. Opinions on the success of ACs were varied but positive views were expressed in companies where the chief executive and senior management backed the idea and the members of the AC had the requisite abilities and commitment. The researchers commented that the effectiveness of ACs depended 'more upon the personalities involved than upon any other variables'.

The 1977 survey showed that 88% of companies had an AC. The significant increase in the number of companies with ACs since the previous study was attributed to the influence of the SEC and the New York Stock Exchange. The composition of ACs was similar to the 1970 study but the breadth of function had widened with greater emphasis on the review of internal audit work and related matters like the discussion of fraud situations and compliance with ethical standards. The opinions on the success of ACs were more equivocal than the previous survey. Concern was expressed over possible interference by ACs into the operational domain but on balance the researchers concluded that ACs can make a contribution to improved corporate governance.

Canada

In early 1970, ACs were virtually unheard of in Canada. For instance, Lam and Arens (1975) reported that in 1971 only 6% of a sample of major Canadian companies had ACs. However, following

31

federal legislation in 1975 and provincial legislation throughout the 1970s, the number of companies with ACs grew. In 1980 a survey (CICA 1981) of a population, which comprised Canada's top 500 companies, large subsidiaries, investment dealers, unincorporated institutions and other companies, found that ACs were widespread. The respondents ranked as the most important objectives of an AC: contact between non-officer directors and external auditors and its' effect on auditor independence; and the provision of a review of audited annual financial statements. The most important functions of ACs were found to be the review of: the audited annual financial statements; accounting principles and policies; problems that the auditors encountered; the meaning and significance of audited figures; and internal controls. Little emphasis was placed on internal audit or wider considerations like compliance with ethical standards.

The mean size of ACs was four members, although almost half the ACs surveyed had three members. In 53% of respondents all members of the AC were non-officer directors. Where officer directors were members they were usually either the chief executive officer and/or the chief finance officer. The majority met two to four times a year for one to three hours. The principal factors for a successful AC, according to respondents, were sound judgement, and independence from management.

The study group strongly supported ACs in appropriate circumstances but considered that the legal requirement should be limited to 'review the annual audited financial statements before approval by the board'. Although additional desirable functions relating to external reporting, external auditors, corporate governance and internal auditors were suggested. The report also concluded that:

the minimum number of members of an AC should be three;

all members of the AC should be independent directors;

officers of the company should be in attendance at AC meetings when required by AC members;

the AC should meet a minimum of two times; and

minutes should be kept and distributed as determined by the board;

International study

As well as questionnaire surveys, the development of the concept of ACs and their formation and development in the US, Canada and the UK was discussed by The Accountants International Study Group (1977). The study observed ACs in the US and Canada have arisen in the wake of financial scandals and litigation against directors. The objective of ACs was to: increase public confidence in the credibility and objectivity of published financial information; to assist directors discharge their financial reporting responsibilities; and strengthen the independence of the corporation's external auditors. The result of the pressures was that an AC is a statutory requirement for most major Canadian corporations (Canadian Business Corporations Act: 1975 and provincial legislation); while in the US, the New York Stock Exchange required a company to have an AC for a Stock Exchange listing. In contrast, in the UK there was no requirement for an AC. The Study Group observed that UK ACs had evolved as an administrative convenience to facilitate main board meetings and that the primary function of the AC was to ensure that the directors prepare financial statements, which show a true and fair view.

The study group found that AC practice was variable especially in the UK where it was wholly unregulated. ACs were established by board resolutions and certainly in the US and Canada consisted wholly or had a majority of non-executive directors. In the UK membership was more mixed and in some ACs executive members predominated. The duties of ACs varied between corporations but generally included reviews of: the audit plan; internal controls; the scope and results of internal audit procedures; the results of the audit; and financial statements. ACs typically met two times a year.

The study group concluded that all publicly owned corporations should establish an AC composed principally of outside directors and that the corporation should disclose the existence and membership of the AC in the annual report.

The surveys that in the UK, US, Canada and by the international study group demonstrate that ACs are fairly homogeneous as regards their composition, procedures and functions. There was widespread support for ACs in companies with ACs and from those who served on or came into contact with ACs.

Research into the effectiveness of ACs

The majority of such research emanates from the US. Examples include:

> Robertson and Deakin (1977) viewed effectiveness in terms of the expertise held and sources of expertise consulted by members of ACs. The approach was to list a series of tasks and inquire whether assistance was required by the AC and if so from where it was obtained. ACs required assistance with a number of matters and relied most upon the external auditors as advisers.

> Grinaker et al (1978) approached the effectiveness problem by asking chief executive officers, chief financial officers, audit partners, heads of internal audit and AC members to rate a number of effectiveness criteria. The diligence of the AC

members was the factor that was most highly correlated with AC effectiveness and was the most dominant characteristic in explaining variations in assessment of overall effectiveness. The knowledge base of the AC was also a highly rated factor.

Reinstein (1980) developed a normative model through translating ten Generally Accepted Auditing Standards into a conceptual framework for the duties and responsibilities of ACs. The results of a questionnaire on the extent to which the AC carried out certain procedures or received certain information led to the conclusion that most ACs were effective in terms of the conceptual framework.

Birkett (1980) asked audit committee members and external auditors to rate the effectiveness of the AC in carrying out certain functions. The external auditors rated effectiveness of the AC at a lower level than did members of the AC but both groups suggested that ACs were reasonably effective in carrying out key functions.

Jackson-Heard (1987) undertook experimental research, which concluded that the AC does enhance the perception of auditors' independence but not to a marked degree.

Knapp (1987) employed an experimental task, that contained various case situations involving conflict between management and auditors. The objective was for respondents to state whether they would support the management or the auditors. The case was mailed in a questionnaire to 500 of the largest publicly owned corporations in California. Two significant results emerged: (i) corporate manager subjects were more supportive of auditors than subjects that were retired business executives or from a non-business background (typically independent director members of an AC); and (ii) subjects were more likely to support the auditor over objective technical standards when the auditee was in poor financial circumstances. The findings suggest that ACs are of limited effectiveness in providing support to auditors in disputes with management.

Kalbers (1989) adopted the premise that AC effectiveness is a function of the power of the AC, where power is the capacity to get things done. The results showed that AC effectiveness is highly associated with 'referent power, expert power, information power, coalition power, and the diligence of ACs'. There was also a strong link between effectiveness and sanctionary power over internal and external auditors.

The evidence obtained from these research projects is equivocal on whether ACs are effective. The results are at variance with the opinions of many respondents with whom the matter was discussed in the course of this research.

Research into why some companies have ACs and others do not

Information on differences between companies with and without ACs was obtained as a by-product of various surveys. For example:

Kunitake (1981) and Campbell (1982) investigated the effect of the AC on the selection of the external auditor and particularly whether firms with ACs changed to 'Big-eight auditors'. No statistically significant results emerged. However, clearer results were obtained by Eichensher and Shields (1985). The researchers compared two groups of American Stock Exchange companies. One group had changed external auditors and the other had not. The researchers found that (i) although all companies that changed auditors tended towards selecting Big-eight auditor's, the trend was more pronounced in companies with ACs; and (ii) companies that changed auditors were more likely subsequently to form an AC if the successor auditor was a Big-eight firm.

Crawford (1987) attempted for a sample of American Stock Exchange companies to identify variables that might explain the presence or absence of an AC. The results showed no support for a link between a company having or not having an AC and the following variables: changes in accounting policy; qualified audit opinions; changes in external auditors and litigation concerning financial reporting involving the directors, officers or auditors.

Pincus et al (1989) used an agency theory framework to analyse the reasons for forming ACs. The resultant hypotheses were examined using a random sample of NASDAQ over-the-counter companies. Six characteristics were found to be associated with the voluntary formation of ACs: (i) lower percentage of managerial ownership; (ii) higher leverage; (iii) larger firm size; (iv) a greater proportion of outside directors to total directors; (v) Big-eight auditors; (vi) participation in the National Market System (therefore among the most actively traded NASDAQ securities).

Bradbury (1990) also used an agency theory framework to determine the incentives for the voluntary formation of ACs. The study also examined the influence of size and the incentives of Big-eight auditors and directors to establish ACs. The research covered 135 firms listed on the New Zealand Stock Exchange. The findings show that the voluntary creation of ACs is not related to auditor incentive variables or agency costs derived from the separation of ownership and control; however there is a relationship between voluntary AC formation and director incentives. Both the number of directors on the board and intercorporate ownership were found to be strongly related to a firm having an AC.

The research findings are contradictory. For example, Bradbury (1990) stated that in a 'purely voluntary environment, very few firms form audit committees'; whereas Pincus (1989) found that 68% of a random sample of US corporations had voluntarily formed an AC. Further, Bradbury disagrees with Eichensher and Shields (1985) and Pincus (1989) in finding no link between Big-eight auditors and the formation of ACs. The explanation may lie in cultural differences between New Zealand and the US or merely relate to the limited coverage of the research.

Summary

There has been extensive research into ACs in the US and Canada. The evidence regarding the spread of ACs throughout major companies in these countries is good but information on the effectiveness of ACs and why some companies have them and others do not is mixed.

Chapter 4

Methodology

The population and sample

The objective of the research was to gauge the present state of ACs in the UK. The original intention was to cover only industrial institutions but, following discussions with the Bank of England, the scope of the project was extended to include financial institutions. As there are differences between the regulatory environment for industrial companies and financial institutions and because the fundamental nature of the businesses are different it was decided to treat industrial concerns and financial institutions as separate populations. Consideration was given to extending the population to include local and central government and other public sector organisations.[15] The extension was not made as it was thought that the governance systems and auditor relationships were sufficiently different from the corporate sector for the results not to be comparable with industrial companies and financial institutions.

---

[15] For example: Low (1988) 'As part of their continuing drive to provide an effective and effective service, internal audit units within central government seek to develop good working relationships with top, senior and lower levels of management. Many units have been instrumental in setting up audit committees as a means of enhancing relationships, particularly with top and senior management.'

From 11 January 1991 a new University Funding Committee Code of Practice for Internal and External Audit requires universities to set up an audit committee to review the effectiveness of the internal audit procedures and recommended the external auditors.

Industrial companies

In order to provide a mix of organisations that were significant in the British economy the Times Top 1000 (Allen 1989) was used. The most recent surveys (Marrian 1988, Bank of England 1988)[16] indicate that large organisations are more likely to have audit committees. Therefore, in order to obtain a high proportion of companies with ACs so that current AC practice could be determined, the population for study was limited to the first 250 organisations in the Times 1000. The organisations were checked for suitability for the purposes of the questionnaire. The criteria were that each organisation was trading and not the subsidiary of another member of the population. Therefore, organisations which had ceased to trade, had been taken over by or were subsidiaries of organisations already on the list, were identified[17] and excluded. This reduced the population to 237 industrial concerns.

---

[16] Marrian (1988) 'The existence of ACs is rather more prevalent in the top 500 rather than The Times top 1000'.

Bank of England (1988) survey found that 38% of The Times 1000 had an AC. However, in The Times Top 250 the percentage with an AC was as high as 56%; whereas it was only 31% in the Times lower 250.

[17] For Example:
'Shell' Transport & Trading (3) and Shell UK (9) and Conoco (UK) (187) and Conoco (94) - duplicated

Electricity Council (4) - defunct

Consolidated Gold Fields (133) and Northern Engineering Inds (172) - taken over by organisations already in the population

Coloroll Group (210) and Polly Peck International (173) - in receivership or being wound up.

To explore the nature of the residual population, the members of the population were classified by status as follows:

(i)   UK listed companies – companies with a UK head office and Stock Exchange listing;

(ii)   Foreign subsidiaries – subsidiaries of corporations based overseas;

(iii)   Public sector organisations; and

(iv)   Other firms – UK companies and other organisations not quoted on a Stock Exchange.

It was decided to sample the entire population. Table 1 analyses the sample according to The Times, position and the status of the entities.

Table 1

Analysis of the Times 250 1989-1990

Position	UK listed companies	Other firms	Foreign subsidiaries	Public sector	Total
Top 50	38	1	6	3	48
51-100	39	1	9	0	49
101-150	35	3	7	2	48
151-200	23	6	17	1	47
201-150	33	1	11	0	45
	168	12	50	6	237

Financial institutions

Financial institutions differ from the industrial companies in terms of tighter regulation and a greater need for public confidence. The population was again defined by reference to the Times 1000 (Allen 1989) lists, which includes details of the largest clearing banks, discount houses, other British banks, finance houses, unit trusts, insurance companies, building societies and investments trusts. The sample again emphasised organisation size and was limited to 50 financial institutions. The institutions selected from the Times 1000 1989-90 comprise:

> The four major London clearing banks;
> the three Scottish clearing banks;
> the top 31 other British banks;[18]
> the six largest building societies; and
> the six largest insurance companies.[19]

Although the sample does not reflect the full diversity of financial institutions the members are major economic entities, which are subject

---

[18] Banks and Security Houses registered in the UK but excluding the clearing banks and their subsidiaries.

[19] Determined according to stock market value at 1 January 1991.

to statutory regulation from external bodies.[20] The sample includes
examples from both the monetary sector and non-bank financial

---

Table 2

Profile of the sample financial institutions

	Status				
Type	UK listed	Foreign subsidiaries	Public sector	Other	Total
Clearing banks (London and Scottish)	6	1	—	—	7
Other British banks	11	14	1	5	31
Insurance companies	6	–	—	—	6
Building societies	–	–	–	6	6
TOTAL	23	15	1	11	50

---

[20] The statutory regulations comprise;
Monetary sector - the Bank of England under the Banking Act 1987 is responsible for supervising institutions in the monetary sector (retail banks, discount houses, foreign banks etc.);

Building societies - the Building Societies Act 1986 established a Building Societies Commission to determine whether or not the conduct of a society's business adheres to the Act.

Insurances companies - the Insurance Companies Act 1982 creates an authorising and monitoring role for the Department of Trade and Industry.

intermediaries. Therefore it is contended that the 50 institutions provide a reasonable basis for examining AC practices in major financial institutions.

Table 2 shows the 50 organisations analysed both by institution type, as discussed above, and by status. The categories of status identified are identical to those used for industrial concerns.

Administration of the questionnaire

The questionnaire and a covering letter were sent to the two samples in January 1991. As recommended by Dillman (1978), two follow-up

Table 3

Timing of responses

	Industrial companies	Response rates % *	Financial institutions	Response rates % *
1st mailing	124	53	30	60
2nd mailing	45	40	9	45
3rd mailing	32	48	5	45
	202		44	

* calculated by reference to the residual population – eg industrial companies second mailing 45/ (237-125).

mailings were sent to non-respondents. The first at the end of February 1991 and the second in the third week of April 1991. In both cases replacement questionnaires were sent and reply-paid envelopes included. The incidence of the resultant responses is shown in Table 3.

The mailings of the questionnaire, follow-ups and the lag of responses mean that the process took almost four months. The response rates for all three mailings were excellent. This reflects: the topicality of ACs and the interest of respondents in the results; and the rewards of persistence.

Response rates

Industrial companies

Full responses were received from 189 organisations giving a useable response rate of 80%. In addition 13 organisations that refused to complete the questionnaire were prepared to indicate whether or not they had an AC. This means that some response was received from 85% of the sample.

Financial institutions

Full responses were received from 42 financial institutions. In addition, one financial institution refused to participate and another provided incomplete information. Both these financial institutions had an AC. This gave an overall response rate of 88% and a useable response rate of 84%.

45

Representativeness of the population

Whenever there is less than 100% response rate there is a danger of non-response bias. According to Wallace and Mellor (1988), three types of checks can be carried out to assess the likelihood of significant bias:

(i)   comparison of the profile of respondents against known population characteristics;

(ii)   comparison of the characteristics of respondents with non-respondents; and

(iii)   comparison of the profiles of 'early' and 'late' respondents on the grounds that late respondents are surrogates for non-respondents.

Industrial companies

The high response rate means that non-response bias should be minimal. However, an analysis of the useable response by Times 250 position and the status of the organisation, as shown in Table 4, indicates that responses are not evenly spread throughout the sample/population.

The results indicate that:

the largest companies have a better response rate than smaller companies; and

responses from UK listed companies and public sector organisations are higher than those from foreign subsidiaries and other organisations.

46

An examination of the sample shows that the two findings are inter-linked since six of the seven 'other' organisations, which have a poor response rate, are in the 101-250 range. Further, UK listed companies, which have a high response rate comprise 79% of the top 100 but only 65% of the 101-250 range. Results on the incidence of ACs, discussed in Chapter 5, indicate that the low response rate from 'other' organisations and foreign subsidiaries may be explained by the absence of ACs in such bodies.

Table 4

Analysis of useable responses and response rates

Times 1000 position	UK listed companies	Foreign subsidiaries	Public sector	Other	Total	% response rate
Top 50	33	6	3		42	88
51-100	36	6		1	43	88
101-150	28	4	3	2	37	77
151-200	20	10	1	4	35	74
201-250	26	6			32	71
Total	143	32	7	7	189	80%
% responses by status	85	64	100	58		80%

47

Given the equivocal results from a comparison of population/sample characteristics, an analysis of 'early' and 'late' responses was undertaken. Early responses were defined as those received from the first mailing and late responses as those received from subsequent mailings. The responses to four questions (covering age of the AC, the number of members of the AC, the number of times the AC met annually and the total number of functions assigned to the AC) were examined and the hypothesis that there is no difference between the means of early and late respondents was tested.[21] In general, the results show that for those respondents with an AC non-response bias is limited provided the assumption, that late responders are a good surrogate for non-responders, holds.

Therefore, non-response bias is unlikely to distort the findings with respect to AC practices, procedures and functions.

---

[21] The null hypothesis is that there is no difference between the means. The assumptions are that the variable itself is approximately normally distributed and that the variances are equal. The results were:

Question	Age	Membership	Meetings	Functions
Mean -early	2.9315	4.8219	2.9178	18.0548
-late	2.5862	4.1429	3.2069	19.5172
F value	1.09	1.29	1.05	1.02
T value*	1.02	1.78	-1.16	-1.05
Degrees of freedom	100	99	100	100
2-tail probability	0.312	0.077	0.248	0.296

*Pooled variance estimate as F value close to one.

For three of the four questions the null hypothesis is sustained. In the case of membership, the null hypothesis would be rejected at the 5% level but not the 10% level.

48

Financial institutions

The high response rate means that non-response bias should be minimal. However, an analysis of the useable responses by type of financial institution and the status of the organisation, as shown in Table 5, indicates that responses are not evenly spread throughout the sample/population.

Table 5

Analysis of useable responses and response rates

Type of financial institution	UK listed companies	Foreign subsidiaries	Public sector	Other	Total	%
Clearing banks (London and Scottish)	6	1	–	–	7	100
Other British banks	10	9	–	5	24	77
Insurance companies	6	–	–	–	6	100
Building societies	–	–	–	5	5	83
	22	10	–	10	42	84%
% response by status	96	67	0	91	84%	

As with industrial companies the results indicate that non-respondents are not evenly spread in the population. Excluding the two incomplete responses, the six non-respondents are five foreign subsidiaries, all in the 'other British banks' category, and an insurance company. The findings of Chapter 6 show that the many foreign subsidiaries did not have ACs and therefore the lack of these respondents is unlikely to distort the results of questions concerning ACs. In conclusion, the high response rate and the nature of non-responses negate the possibility of non-response bias.

The questionnaire

One questionnaire (see Appendix 1) was administered to both industrial companies and financial institutions. A copy of the questionnaire is included in Appendix 1. The questionnaire comprised 33 questions and yielded over 120 variables for statistical analysis. The questionnaire was actually two questionnaires: one for firms without an AC and the other for those with an AC. The split was achieved with question 1 'Does your organisation have an AC'. No attempt was made to define an AC in order to obtain as wide a coverage as possible. The definition of an AC for the research, as discussed in Chapter 1, was obtained by checking question 9 to see if there were any non-executive directors on the AC and question 22 to ensure that the AC was involved in some aspects of the audit. Those without an AC answered only questions 2 to 4 yielding a minimum of eight variables for analysis. Organisations with an AC completed questions 5 to 33 generating over 110 variables on the nature of their AC.

The questions were a mix of close-ended and partially open-ended questions with ordered answer choices in as many questions as possible. The questionnaire was 12 pages long including a front and back page. The length was limited by the comments of Dillman

(1978)[22]. Every effort was made to produce a questionnaire that was attractive, well organised and easy to complete. Specifically considered during the design were factors like:

> ordering of the questions – commencing with the easy questions, which are clearly related to the topic at the start and questions on factual information (like number of shareholders, which may need to be looked up, at the end).
> establishing a vertical flow – with response categories following below questions where possible to give a good appearance and avoid omissions in answering.

> clear directions on how questions should be answered.

> making questions fit pages – to minimise confusion and errors and enhance the appearance of the document.

> design of the front sheet to give prominence to the prestigious names linked with the project.

The questions, following question 1, fell into three groups:

> Factual information with no guidance as to the response – questions 4 and 33 asked for the approximate number of shareholders in the organisation. The question was duplicated in order to obtain the information for all respondents irrespective of whether or not they had an AC. Question 6 sought information about other ACs in the group and questions 9, 10, 17 and 18 obtained information on the membership of the AC, and details

---

[22] Dillman (1978:55) stated that 'going beyond 12 pages seems almost certain to affect responses....thus we tentatively conclude that 11 pages, or 125 items, represent plateaus beyond which response rate reductions can be expected.'

of AC meetings. Finally question 31 asked for information on the age of the AC for comparison with results of Chambers and Snook (1979) and Marrian (1988).

Factual information with guidance as to the response - the guidance was to answer yes or no except for question 11, concerning the duration of appointments to the AC, where a series of possibilities were provided. Question 6 asked whether or not there were other ACs in the group. Questions 12 to 16 and 19 to 21 sought information on AC practices and procedures. Question 22 enquired which of a list of 32 functions were assigned to ACs, question 23 allowed respondents to identify any omitted items and question 24 adopted an alternative approach by requesting respondents to identify and rank the five most important functions in each of four areas. Finally question 30 sought to establish disclosure practices regarding ACs. Three disclosure levels were identified: existence, objectives and functions and identity of the AC members. The disclosure levels sought are less than those proposed by the Macdonald Commission CICA (1987). The commission report suggested that not only should the directors publish a formal statement of the responsibilities assigned to shareholders, but that ACs should also report annually to the shareholders on the manner in which they have fulfilled this mandate.

Opinion gathering questions – questions 2, 7, 25, 27 and 29 – sought to gauge the levels of agreement of respondents to a selection of matters concerning ACs. The questions listed predetermined possibilities, although respondents were given the opportunity to identify additional possibilities in questions 3, 8, 26 and 28. Questions 2 and 3 explored possible motives for an organisation not having an AC. The seven motives listed were obtained from discussion and the literature from professional bodies and accounting firms (for example: AISG 1977; CICA

1981; Peat Marwick McLintock 1987; and Coopers & Lybrand Deloitte 1990). Questions 7 and 8 discuss the motives for an organisation having an AC. The 13 motives listed were obtained from the same source as the motives for not having an AC. Questions 25 and 27 concerning, respectively, the attributes of members and practices, which contributed to AC success were based on discussion with firms with ACs and similar questions in Mautz and Neuman (1976) and CICA (1981). Question 29 involved three contentious statements. The first two statements concerned ACs using outside technical specialists or internal audit staff in the course of discharging their responsibilities. The third question involved the imposition of ACs by legislation as occurs in Singapore, certain provinces in Canada and was recommended by the Macdonald Commission (CICA 1989).

The extent of agreement was ascertained using a five point Likert scale, where 1 'indicates 'strongly agree' and 5 means 'strongly disagree'. The use of the Likert scale presupposes that respondents have stable perceptions and consensual cognition (or common understanding) of the items under discussion and any results must be interpreted with this caveat.

Respondents were also asked to give their name and position.

Additional procedures

Pretesting

The questionnaire was extensively pretested. Three main pretest groups were selected and asked to identify any problems with the draft questionnaire and covering letter (for example, inappropriate terms, confusing words, missing possibilities and inappropriate sequencing of items). The groups were:

colleagues – fellow academics with an interest in the questionnaire design or the area;

companies with an AC; and

people outside organisations with an AC, who had an interest in the area including audit partners and representatives of the sponsoring body.

The questionnaire underwent seven revisions as a result of the pretesting process before an agreed version was accepted by the sponsoring body.

Validation

The questionnaire results were validated through discussion with some 30 respondents in industrial companies and banks. The validation centred on all abnormal responses, companies that had not fully completed the questionnaire and a number of other organisations, which were selected so as to cover the range of organisations in the samples. Some of these organisations contributed to longer discussions on AC matters.

Summary

The research focuses on two separate populations identified by reference to the Times 1000 1989-1990. The populations are large industrial organisations and major financial institutions. A common questionnaire was sent to the Times top 250 industrial concerns and major financial institutions. The latter comprised all the clearing banks, the largest 'other British banks', the largest insurance companies and the largest building societies.
The response rates achieved were excellent. The overall response rate

was 85% for industrial companies and 88% for financial institutions. An analysis of non-responses indicated that non-responses arose principally among organisations which were less likely to have ACs. It was concluded that there was a minimal chance of non-response bias in assessing the results of the questionnaire.

The excellent response was attributed to careful questionnaire design, thorough pretesting and the topicality of corporate governance.

Chapter 5

Audit Committees in Industrial Companies

The numbers of organisations with an AC

Full responses were received from 189 organisations (80% of the sample). In addition 13 organisations that refused to complete the questionnaire were prepared to indicate whether or not they had an AC. Therefore information on the presence of an AC was available from 202 organisations (85% of the sample). Table 1 shows the number of organisations with an AC analysed by the Times 1000 with respect to position and organisation status.

Table 1

Number of industrial companies with an AC

Times 1000 position	Replies	With an AC	No AC	% of replies with an AC
Top 50	43	24	19	56
51-100	46	28	18	61
101-150	40	24	16	60
151-200	37	16	21	43
201-250	36	16	20	44
Total	202	108	94	53%

Status of respondents	Replies	With an AC	No AC	% of replies with an AC
UK listed companies	150	97	53	65
Other firms	7	1	6	14
Foreign subsidiaries	38	4	34	10
Public sector organisations	7	6	1	86
Overall	202	108	94	53%

The results suggest that ACs are widespread but not universally adopted. The analysis by organisation size as measured by Times 1000 position reveals some link between size and the existence of an AC since 59% of the top 150 organisations have an AC against 44% of the organisations in positions 151-250. However, the link is not statistically significant.[23] Part of the explanation for the finding lies in the fact that 79% of the top 150 respondents are quoted UK based companies (which have a high incidence of ACs) against 66% of respondents in the 151-250 group. The highest incidence of ACs was in public sector organisations. Clearly there is a connection between organisational

[23] For Times top 250 position, the hypothesis of no association is accepted. Chi-squared value 4.331 with 4 degrees of freedom compared to a critical value of 9.49 at 95% confidence.

status and the existence of an AC[24] with the incidence of ACs varying widely between different status categories.

In discussions with respondents in public sector organisations, the following reasons were advanced for the almost universal adoption of ACs:

> public sector bodies follow best practice in the corporate sector;

> the responsibility for public money requires strong controls and effective audit, which are supported by the AC;

> the non-executive directors have a special responsibility as representatives of the public for the scrutiny of management's performance in safeguarding public funds. The AC is an ideal vehicle for facilitating this task; and

> a tendency for such organisations to bureaucracy.

It was also noted that all privatised organisations which responded to the questionnaire had an AC. This suggests that the AC is still seen to be useful despite the absence of the special circumstances surrounding public sector bodies. ACs were present in the majority of UK quoted companies and infrequent in foreign subsidiaries and other firms. This represents a considerable increase in the number of ACs since Chambers and Snook (1979), which for a parallel sample found 13% of firms had ACs, and Marrian (1988), which in a 1985 survey of the Times 1000 reported that 17% of respondents had ACs. Both surveys reported that ACs were a relatively recent phenomenon with the majority of ACs being formed in the three years preceding the

---

[24] For organisation status, the hypothesis of no association is rejected. Chi-squared value 42.7914 with 3 degrees of freedom compared to a critical value of 7.82 at 95% confidence.

research. A similar finding is derived from the 99 respondents that provided information on the age of their AC. This suggests that the formation of ACs by major concerns has continued throughout the eighties. The age distribution of the ACs surveyed is shown in Table2.

Table 2

Age of ACs

Years	Number of respondents	% of respondents
0-2	21	21
3-5	31	32
6-8	16	16
9-11	13	13
12-14	10	10
15 and over	8	8
	99	100

The Table shows that ACs are a relatively new phenomenon with over half being established in the five years since January 1986 and a fifth in the two years preceding January 1991. There are some long established ACs with five respondents reporting that their AC was over 20 years old.

An analysis comparing the age of ACs and the size of organisations as determined by Times position suggests that there is a link between age and organisation size.[25] Table 3 shows that the oldest ACs are present in the largest companies. Over half the Top 50 companies are over nine years old, whereas none of the AC committees in the Times 201-250 are over five years old.

Table 3

Age of ACs analysed by Times 1000 position

| Years | Times position | | | | |
	Top 50	51-100	101-150	151-200	201-250
0-2	2	4	7	3	5
3-5	3	6	8	7	7
6-8	6	6	1	3	–
9-11	4	7	1	1	–
12-14	4	2	4	–	–
15 and over	4	1	1	1	1
	23	26	22	15	13

[25] The hypothesis of no association is rejected. Chi-squared value 32.62 with 20 degrees of freedom compared to a critical value of 31.41 at 95% confidence level.

Of the respondents with an AC, 19% reported that there were other audit committees in the group. Table 4 analyses the existence of multiple ACs by organisation status and Times position.

Table 4

Incidence of multiple ACs

| Organisation status | Times position | | | | | |
	Top 50	51-100	101-150	151-200	201-250	Total
Other firms	–	–	–	–	–	–
UK listed companies	8	3	4	–	2	17
Foreign subsidiaries	–	1	1	–	–	2
Public sector organisations	–	–	–	–	–	–
Total	8	4	5	–	2	19

Multiple ACs were most frequent in UK listed companies in the Times Top 50. The number of additional ACs among UK listed companies ranged from one to seven with a mean of 2.9 other ACs. The most frequently mentioned locations were the US, Canada, Australia and New Zealand. The US was cited by 76% of respondents with other ACs. The two foreign subsidiaries, which reported the existence of multiple ACs in the group were both owned by firms on the North American continent. The UK ACs were the only other AC in the group apart from the head office AC; and one of three other ACs under the group AC.

Reasons given for multiple ACs included: an overseas subsidiary with strong regional associations; safeguarding minority interest in partially owned subsidiaries; part of an overall control structure covering business units; and conforming with local practice in the US and Canada.

In eight (42%) cases there was no link or inter-relationship between the main AC and other ACs in the group. The commonest method followed by 45% of respondents with multiple ACs was for subsidiary ACs to submit reports to the group board or AC. Other methods mentioned included: common guidelines for role, terms of reference, charter and working methods; group AC has a watching brief over subsidiary ACs and reviews minutes; and via group internal audit. The institutions without links gave reasons like: the lack of materiality of the unit with an AC; a willingness to delegate local corporate governance decisions to subsidiaries; and a common firm of external auditors.

Reasons for an organisation not having an AC

Organisations without an AC were asked to indicate, using a scale from 1 meaning strongly agree to 5 representing strongly disagree, the extent to which they concur with a number of possible reasons for the organisation not having an AC. Table 5 lists the seven reasons included in the questionnaire in order of the extent of agreement as determined by the mean score of responses. Information on the standard deviation (std dev) is given to indicate the relative dispersion of the responses.

Table 5

Reasons for not having an AC

	Mean	Std dev
ACs are merely additional bureaucracy	2.49	1.19
The cost of an AC outweighs the benefits	2.79	1.33
ACs act as a barrier between the auditor and the main board	2.92	1.24
No legal requirement	3.08	1.51
ACs create conflict within the organisation	3.22	1.23
ACs have no teeth	3.24	1.06
ACs are a first step to two tier boards	3.27	1.32

The results reveal little consensus on the reasons for not having an AC. The means varied from 2.49 to 3.27 compared with the scale mean of 3. The maximum proportion of respondents indicating strong agreement with any of the reasons given was 20% for 'ACs are merely additional bureaucracy' and maximum percentage for strongly disagree was 30% for the reason 'no legal requirement'. The latter reason showed the greatest variation in opinion; 42% of respondents agreed to an extent with the proposition to offset the responses indicating strong disagreement. This reflects the following two contrary views amongst respondents: (i) if there was a legal requirement then the firm

63

would have an AC; and (ii) if ACs were beneficial the firm would have an AC irrespective of the legal situation.

Respondents were asked to indicate whether there were any reasons, beyond those listed, why the organisations did not have an AC. Over 50 reasons were mentioned. The reasons can be considered under four headings.

Inappropriate

It was deemed inappropriate to have an AC for a number of reasons:

(i) a number of the organisations, that were foreign subsidiaries or unlisted companies, stated that it was inappropriate for such organisations to have an AC. Examples of the reasons given for an AC being inappropriate included: a statement that 'An AC is not appropriate for the company as it is the wholly owned subsidiary of a foreign (US) corporation. The parent corporation, however, has an AC'; another foreign subsidiary stated that it was 'not appropriate to have an AC at subsidiary level'; and two private companies indicated that ACs were 'not relevant to our type of organisation'. This link between the status of an organisation and the establishment of an AC was emphasised by one respondent with the reply 'We became listed last year and will be creating an AC shortly'.

(ii) the absence of a formal internal audit department was viewed as removing the need for an AC. A large subsidiary of a US multinational responded thus: 'we are a private company with no internal audit function therefore an audit committee is unnecessary'. While a UK listed company answered 'We have no formal internal audit structure and therefore no need of an AC'.

(iii) in some organisations ACs were inappropriate because they were unnecessary. Reasons for this attitude include: 'full board considers relevant matters'; 'the group has strong system of internal control and its' own internal audit department'; 'the external auditor attends relevant board meetings and informally meets all board members fairly regularly, so a formal structure is not deemed necessary'; 'our non-executive directors have unfettered access to our auditors'; 'the objectives of the AC can with a relatively small board be better achieved with internal and external auditors reporting to the full board' and 'calibre of non-executive directors make an audit committee unnecessary'. Finally a number of respondents suggested that ACs were window dressing and a means of avoiding crucial issues. This view is summed up by the following response 'audit committees are no substitute for strong financial control, good internal audit with access to independent directors within an organisation where standard and integrity are paramount'. Many of these latter examples correspond with the alternative to ACs specified in ICAEW (1991).

Detrimental

ACs were seen by a number of respondents as being detrimental to the organisation. Six respondents believed that ACs were detrimental as the AC breaches the principle of collective board responsibility in the extremely important areas of internal control, audit and financial reporting. The opinion is perhaps best summarised by the statement of one company that 'the board fulfils the role and responsibilities of the AC, which should not be delegated'. Other detrimental effects of ACs mentioned by respondents included: 'our non-executive directors believe them to be a waste of time'; 'audit committees detract from strong financial management'; 'ACs are counter productive'; and, audit committees remove openness between auditors and directors since the interface between the auditors and the full board is removed.

Difficulties

ACs were viewed by some respondents as posing difficulties for the organisation. Several respondents stated that they did not have sufficient non-executive directors or non-executive directors with the relevant skills and interest to form an AC or that the board was too small. For example Thorn EMI plc in their 1991 annual report in a section on 'Corporate Governance' stated 'Thorn EMI's board is small and does not have a separate audit committee. However I[26] take the chair for discussion of the audit, and separately and independently discuss the results with our Auditors. I am therefore able to satisfy myself about regulatory and statutory compliance and any significant change in accounting practice'. Others responded that non-executive directors on ACs rarely have sufficient time to make the AC effective. One respondent indicated that he would anticipate that with preparation, meetings and travel it would probably require up to 100 hours per annum for each director – a significant additional commitment. Another difficulty suggested by four respondents was that 'corporate culture is not yet ready for an AC'. One respondent indicated that the corporate ethos was to avoid unnecessary formalisation and bureaucracy and minimise administration overheads and that an AC would be perceived as running counter to these aims.

Inertia

Several respondents indicated that the status quo was satisfactory and that there was no reason to introduce an AC. A typical comment made by the finance director of a listed company was that 'present auditor board communications are deemed satisfactory and therefore there is no pressure for change'. Others indicated that the benefits of ACs

---

[26] Deputy chairman and non-executive director.

were not fully appreciated by them. Finally one company indicated that it was a case of priorities.

One respondent indicated that the company had an AC until the mid-1980s but it was 'so useless' that it was disbanded. The finance director of the company said that the non-executive directors had expressed relief at the demise of the AC. The closure reflected a belief that the AC makes no money for the organisation and that ACs and external auditors fail to address the real areas of risk in a business. The attitude of the firm to ACs was summed up by the remark that 'when the Japanese require their companies to have ACs, we will have one'.

Seven respondents indicated that arrangements existed, which, although they did not amount to a formally constituted AC, fulfilled all or part of the role of an AC. The nature of these 'quasi ACs' were as follows:

A major public company had an AC consisting of the chief executive, three other executives and the audit partners. The AC provides an interface between group management and external auditors and deals with internal controls, auditing and financial reporting. The approach has been in operation since the 1960s and is perceived as having worked well.

Another major public company replied that, although there was no formal AC, there was a close working relationship with external auditors. The chairman and finance director have regular discussions with group audit partners and likewise at divisional level. There is consultation with the auditors on accounting and other matters of principle prior to making financial decisions, which have accounting implications. Further, as there is no group internal audit department, great stress is put on the actioning of management letters.

A similar situation exists at a smaller public company. The chairman and chief executive invite the external auditors regularly to review the annual accounts, review accounting principles and practice, discuss internal controls with the external auditors and the results of their audit of the accounts and enquire into illegal or unethical acts.

A fourth company operates 'an effective Internal Control Management Process, which *inter alia* performs some of the functions normally attributed to audit committees'. For example reviewing the adequacy of internal controls and the scope and results of the work of the internal and external auditors.

The 'quasi AC' in another company took the form of alternative arrangements where the external auditors reported separately to the non-executive directors. The company described the arrangement as 'performing most of the AC functions.'

At a major foreign subsidiary there was an AC comprising the executive directors in charge of marketing, manufacturing, personnel, finance, legal matters and the chairman. The AC considered all aspects of the internal auditor's work and had as a key objective 'increasing the profile of internal auditors within the organisation'. The approach stemmed partly from an 'awareness of the business benefits that accrue from a skilled internal audit group'.

Finally, one public company created a monthly liaison through non-executive directors and executives having unlimited access to the chief executive officer and chief financial officer, the business heads and auditors as required. The company stated that there was no pressure from non-executive directors for an instrument they see as being additional bureaucracy.

The motives for having an AC

Respondents were asked to indicate a scale from 1 (strongly agree) to 5 (strongly disagree) the extent to which they agreed that 13 reasons reflect the motives for having an AC in the organisation. Table 6 lists the 13 reasons in order of the extent of agreement as determined by the mean score of responses. Information on the standard deviation (std dev) is given to indicate the relative dispersion of the responses.

The two motives for establishing ACs, which gained the highest level of agreement as measured by the mean score, were 'good corporate practice', which was clearly the dominant motive with 76% indicating strong agreement, and 'strengthens the role and effectiveness of non-executive directors', which had 55% of respondents with an AC agreeing strongly with this motive. These motives do not stress direct benefits through meeting the objectives of ACs like improved financial reporting and more independent auditing; rather the motives reveal a general acceptance that ACs are a 'good thing' and have a key role in integrating non-executive directors (another good corporate practice). The finance director of one UK quoted company illustrated this point by stating that the idea for setting up an AC followed logically from the introduction of non-executive directors to the board. Actions like this suggest that recent publications, which have emphasised the contribution that ACs and non-executive directors can make to corporate governance (see for example ICAEW 1991 or Coopers & Lybrand Deloitte 1990), have led to a general acceptance of their benefits. The motive with the next highest strongly agree rating was 'assists directors in discharging their statutory responsibilities as regards financial reporting' (52%). This reflects the increased awareness among directors of their responsibilities in this area and the decision by many boards to delegate the examination of such matters to a subcommittee of the board, which can ensure that greater attention is paid to these matters. Interestingly, the communications with and the independence of internal auditors was rated above the same motives for external auditors in explaining the existence of an AC.

Table 6

Motives for having an AC

Reasons		Mean	Std dev
1.	good corporate practice	1.31	0.61
2.	strengthens the role and effectiveness of non-executive directors	1.58	0.86
3.	assists directors in discharging their statutory responsibilities as regards financial reporting	1.65	0.86
4.	preserves and enhances the independence of internal auditors	1.88	0.87
5.	assists the auditors in the reporting of serious deficiencies in the control environment or management weaknesses	2.08	1.05
6.	improves communications between the board and internal auditors	2.12	0.97
6.	improves communications between the board and external auditors	2.13	0.99
8.	preserves and enhances the independence of external auditors	2.46	1.28
9.	increases the confidence of the public in the credibility and objectivity of financial statements	2.54	1.03

10.	assists management to discharge its responsibilities for the prevention of fraud, other irregularities and errors	2.59	1.15
11.	increases the confidence of investment analysts in the credibility and objectivity of financial statements	2.95	1.13
12.	provides a forum for arbitration between management and auditors	3.35	1.19
13.	possibility of legislative pressure	3.36	1.15

As might have been expected, since the list of reasons given were deliberately plausible, all but two of the motives had a mean below the scale average of 3 indicating some level of mean agreement. The motives with a mean above 3 were those relating to the possibility of legal pressure and the AC as a forum for arbitrating disputes between management and the auditors. The lack of significant aversion of these motives is indicated by only around a fifth of respondents replying that they strongly disagree. The highest level of disagreement (21%) was against the motive 'possibility of legislative pressure'. This is partly explained by the view of some respondents that legislation to impose ACs is highly unlikely and anyway there was no reason, beyond the benefits derived from ACs, to comply in advance.

Respondents were asked to indicate whether there were any other motives, which led to the establishment of an AC. The most frequently mentioned motives included:

US influence

Two companies indicated that their AC was established to comply with New York Stock Exchange listing requirements. Others indicated

71

that the multinational nature of their groups had led them to follow US good practice and establish ACs.

Corporate governance issues

Two companies cited 'broad corporate governance issues' as an important motivation for establishing ACs. Three other organisations had established ACs to improve the efficiency of main board meetings, which were lengthening. The discussion of detailed accounting and auditing matters in the AC results in appreciable time savings. ACs were also seen as important as an internal discipline on the executive and a means of ensuring that action is taken to improve internal controls. Finally, four organisations indicated that motives for forming an AC included providing a forum for the non-executive directors to become more conversant with the business and giving the non-executive directors a formal role.

Auditing benefits

Respondents listed a range of benefits for internal and external auditors from having an AC. Examples of the motives cited include: helps control external auditors, especially as regards fees and the scope of the audit; a forum for examining the effectiveness audits; a means of enhancing the standard of internal auditors in their own eyes and those of their colleagues; and improves communication and collaboration between internal auditors and external auditors. In a wider context, one public sector organisation had an AC as a forum for examining value for money initiatives and stressed the role of the AC in identifying key business controls.

Role in ethical issues

The AC provides a forum for reviewing the content and implementation of a corporate code of practice.

Support for the finance director

The AC can support the finance director in disputes over resources to provide adequate internal controls and in changing accounting policies.

From discussions with respondents it was apparent that factors could act as catalysts to the formation of ACs. Examples of these influences include:

> financial difficulties leading to a review of financial controls and subsequent pressure from bankers, auditors and others for an AC;

> influence from newly acquired companies nationally and internationally that have ACs. Also pressure from non-executive directors with experience of ACs elsewhere; and

> evolution of board structure leading to a split in the finance committee with the AC adopting the audit and reporting functions.

AC practices and procedures

The questionnaire sought to determine the membership structure of ACs: 54 organisations (53%) had an AC composed solely of non-executive directors; five organisations (5%) had non-executive directors and other members on the AC; 34 organisations (33%) had executive and non-executive directors on the AC; and nine organisations (9%) had an AC comprising all three categories of members. The maximum number of members of an AC was 11 (the chairman and chief executive plus nine non-executive directors) at a UK listed company, although another unlisted company[27] had nine (the managing director and eight non-executive directors). In both instances all the non-executive directors were on the AC. The minimum number on an AC was two (both non-executive directors). Table 7 shows the distribution of membership of the respondents' ACs analysed by the categories established. In examining the figures, it must be remembered that in some organisations the finance director and/or representatives of the external auditors and/or the Head of Internal Audit were members of the AC, whereas in other organisations they were not members but merely in attendance. The two most commonly reported compositions of ACs were three non-executive directors (22% of respondents) and four non-executive directors (16% of respondents).

The findings when compared to Chambers and Snook (1979) and Marrian (1988) suggest that the composition and number of members of ACs has altered little. The main change is between Chambers and Snook (1979), who described a typical AC as comprising four members of whom one was an executive director, and Marrian (1988), who found a similar average size but reported that 65% of the ACs were composed solely of non-executive members. This trend towards non-executive membership does not appear to have accelerated over the last six years as this survey found only 53% of ACs were composed solely of non-executive directors. The problem may be one of definition as 69% of respondents' ACs had no executive directors as members.

The executive directors typically included one or more of: the finance director; the chairman; the deputy chairman; and chief executive. Other members were normally the external audit partner/s but others

---

[27] Although the company is unlisted, there are several thousand shareholders and therefore it attempts to conform to listed company behaviour. The non-executive directors on the AC comprise family shareholder representatives and a couple of independent directors.

specified included: head of internal audit; financial controller, group chief accountant and the company secretary.

Table 7

Number of members of ACs

	0	1-2	3-4	5-6	7-8	9-11	Mean	Std dev
					Number			
Executive directors	59	36	7	–	–	–	0.69	0.97
Non-executive directors	–	14	68	18	1	2	3.67	1.29
Other members	86	11	3	–	–	–	0.30	0.89
Total membership	–	3	53	36	6	2	4.66	1.69

Table 8 shows that directors are normally appointed to the AC for an indefinite term. One explanation for this is that non-executive directors with an interest in the area are not numerous enough to permit rotation. Although several respondents mentioned that indefinite 'does not mean without end' and that the position is reviewed when directors retire by rotation. In situations where all non-executive directors are automatically members of the AC the term will be indefinite as long as the non-executive director is a board member.

75

In discussions with respondents it was the general opinion that an indefinite term of membership has benefits. AC members with indefinite membership have an opportunity to see internal control and reporting issues in a longer perspective, develop relevant expertise and appreciate the key issue. One finance director stated that the prime benefit of continuity of membership was the time saved in introducing matters for discussion at AC meetings. However, when pressed some respondents opined that indefinite membership can reduce the essential independence and questioning role of the AC as past decisions become binding precedents.

Table 8

Normal term of the appointment of a director to the AC

	Number of respondents	% of responses
One year	3	3
Two years	2	2
Three years	9	9
Four or five years	4	4
Indefinite	84	82
	102	100

Table 9 shows that in the majority of cases both executive director members (74%) and non-executive director members (57%) of the AC were selected by the board. The mechanics of selection varied but typically the finance director might propose members for approval by the board or the finance director might suggest members to the chairperson who would propose them for ratification by the board. In three organisations, executive directors are, by virtue of holding a particular position (eg chairman or finance director) automatically members. In 16 instances, where board resolutions, the terms of reference or the charter of the AC stated that all non-executive directors were to be on the AC, the selection was also automatic. In all but two instances, the appointments to the AC, if not made by the board, were ratified by the board.

Table 9

Selection of AC members

	Number of respondents			
	Executive directors	%	Non-executive directors	%
By all the board	32	74	59	57
By the chairman	3	7	21	20
By the board and chairperson	–	–	1	1
By a committee of the board	5	12	5	5
Automatically	3	7	16	16
By board and AC chairperson	–	–	1	1
	43	100	102	100

Table 10 reveals that the main bar to a board member serving on an AC is being an executive director. This reflects the policy in the majority of respondents with ACs of limiting membership to non-executive directors. The debarring of persons with a specific office from membership of the AC relates to limitations on which executive directors may be members. The most frequently cited example was a bar on the chairperson being a member. The failure to debar from service board members with shares or stock in the organisation is to be anticipated since the work of the AC does not necessarily run counter

Table 10

Conditions debarring a board member from serving on the AC

	Number of respondents	%
Holding a substantial amount of shares or loan stock in the company	4	4
Holding some shares or loan stock in the company	3	3
Holding a specific office	13	13
Being an executive director	57	56
A lack of financial, accounting or audit knowledge	5	5
No bars	27	26

to the interests of individuals with a material holding in shares or loan stock and certainly do not affect those with less significant holdings. Other comments on the composition of ACs included: no specific bars but non-executive directors preferred; always a majority of non-executive directors; and attempt to combine a balance of those with and without accounting skills.

Only 5% of respondents felt that a lack of financial, accounting or audit knowledge was a bar to a board member serving on an AC. It was generally agreed that the AC should include at least one non-executive member with interests and abilities in relevant areas. Otherwise, other executive or non-executive directors require no specialist abilities; although it is probable that such members would have a broad knowledge of accounting, auditing and controls.

Of respondents with an AC, 51% reported that the chairperson of the AC is selected by the board. Other methods cited by over 10% of respondents were selection by the AC (23%) and selected by the main board chairman or deputy chairman (11%). In the latter case the selection was often ratified by the board. There were only five instances of chairpersons or finance directors being ex officio chairpersons. Respondents emphasised that it was important to control selection of the chairman to maintain the independence of the AC.

The AC secretary was the company secretary, assistant company secretary or nominee of the company secretary in 72% of respondents with an AC. Others reported as holding the post by more than five respondent were: the finance director/financial controller (six instances) and the head of internal audit/director of audit (seven instances).

The frequency of AC meetings did not vary greatly. The majority of respondents (82%) reported that their ACs only held regular meetings. Amongst the reasons given for special meetings were: to review defence or takeover documents; to consider a change in auditors; and to receive special reports from the internal auditors and external auditors. Table 11 shows the frequency of annual AC meetings.

Table 11

Frequency of AC meetings each year

	Number					
	0	1-2	3-4	Over 4	Mean	Std dev
Regular meetings	1	45	51	5	2.77	1.04
Special meetings	82	19	1	–	0.30	0.74
Total annual meetings	–	37	55	10	3.07	1.12

The most commonly occurring number of meetings was two, which was reported by 35 respondents (34%). The meetings were typically held half-yearly and considered the interim and final accounts and matters related thereto. The maximum number of meetings was six being two regular meetings plus four special meetings for quarterly reports. The maximum number of regular meetings was five and the maximum number of special meetings was four.

The duration of meetings showed little variation amongst respondents. The maximum average duration of a meeting was four hours, although one respondent stated that a particular meeting had lasted nearly six hours, and the minimum average duration of a meeting was half an hour. Regular meetings had a mean average duration of around two hours and special meetings had a mean average duration of 1.65 hours.

The shortest average annual duration of AC meetings was two hours (two meetings of an hour) reported by two organisations and the longest was 16 hours (four meetings of four hours) at a UK quoted company, which had in the past been in some financial difficulties. The overall mean average annual duration was 6.5 hours but there was considerable difference between UK quoted companies (mean 8.2 hours) and the other groups (mean 5.8 hours). It was pointed out by respondents in discussions that, as with other committees, meeting time does not equate with the coverage of matters in the meeting. The quality of the briefing papers, the time the members spend in preparation and the quality of the chairmanship all contribute to the productivity of a meeting. Therefore a short formal meeting does not necessarily equate with the tasks of the AC being done in a cursory fashion, although AC efficiency is unlikely to make a disparity of between two and 16 hours.

The results reveal little change since Chambers and Snook (1979) and Marrian (1988). These surveys found that the typical AC had two to three meetings per year which had durations of some two to three hours. Several respondents with whom this was discussed suggested that the time available from non-executive directors was the limiting factor.

The duties and functions of all but four of the ACs were formally stated in some form. Table 12 shows how the duties and responsibilities were specified.

Of respondents with ACs, 60% have the duties and responsibilities of the AC formalised by written terms of reference (see Appendix 2 for an example), 50% of respondents have the duties and responsibilities specified in board resolutions and 35% obtain information on their duties and responsibilities from multiple sources. Only 9% of ACs received their duties and responsibilities from a separate charter. The level of detail on the duties and responsibilities of ACs in board resolutions, written terms of reference and charters varied widely.

Table 12

Specification of the duties and responsibilities of the AC

	Number of respondents	%
Board resolutions	20	20
Board resolutions and a separate charter	4	4
Written terms of reference	29	30
Written terms of reference and board resolutions	23	24
A separate charter and written terms of reference	4	4
Board resolutions, written terms of reference and informal agreement	2	2
An informal agreement	13	13
Other*	3	3
	98	100

*Other comprises:
1. paper agreed by the board and informal agreement.
2. specified in annual report section on board committees.
3. separate charter.

Minutes were produced for audit committee meetings by all the respondents. The minutes were widely distributed as is illustrated in Table 13. It appears to be common for minutes to be distributed to members of the AC, members of the board and external auditors. The minutes distributed to the board were an important means of communicating the deliberations of the AC to the board and even in organisations that did not distribute minutes to all board members; there was an oral report from the AC chairman to the board. As a finance director commented 'the board members do not escape responsibility for the audit and accounts by merely delegating them to a committee; the board must monitor and question AC deliberations and decisions'.

Table 13

Distribution of the minutes

	Number of respondents	% of respondents
Members of the committee	92	90
Board members	85	83
External auditors	82	80
Internal auditors	52	51
Senior management	27	26
Those in attendance	76	75

Note: Two respondents did not give any details
Four respondents stated that a specific report was made to the Board after each AC meeting

Functions assigned to ACs

Respondents were asked to indicate which of 32 possible functions, analysed into the categories – external reporting (eight functions); external auditors (nine functions); internal auditors (eight functions); and other matters (seven functions) – were assigned to ACs in their organisation. Table 14 shows the mean, and standard deviation (std dev) of the number of functions within each of the four categories.

Table 14

Number of functions

	Mean	Std dev
External reporting	4.99	1.89
External audit	5.92	1.82
Internal audit*	6.29	2.10
Other matters	2.42	1.95
Total	18.47	6.34

*Based on the 82 respondents with an internal audit function

The mean of almost 20 functions suggests that a widely varying range of functions are assigned to ACs by organisations. This is especially true of external and internal auditing. For external auditing, although only 10% of respondents reported all nine functions, over three-quarters had five or more of the functions assigned. While for internal auditing almost half the ACs with an internal audit function (43%) assigned all eight of the functions and 82% had five or more functions assigned. The large number of internal audit functions in the organisations surveyed was cited, in discussions with several respondents, as an indication of the importance of links between the internal auditors and the AC in enhancing the status of internal auditors and in stressing their importance in maintaining a sound control environment. External reporting had 10% of respondents assigning all eight functions and 60% with five or more of the functions. However, there were a number of organisations (especially other organisations, public sector bodies and some foreign subsidiaries) where the number of external reporting functions assigned were much lower due to functions like interim reports, Stock Exchange requirements and circulars on takeovers being irrelevant to the situation. Other matters covered seven examples of the wider functions which may be given to ACs. Only 16 respondents assigned five or more of the seven functions listed and 72% had three or less. This indicates that ACs are largely concerned with financial reporting and auditing. The wide differences in the functions of ACs is indicated by the range of the total number of functions assigned to ACs, which were from 3 (a tenth of the 32 listed) to 32 and the standard deviation of over six. There was no pattern to explain the number of functions either in terms of the status or industry group of the respondents.

Discussions with a number of the respondents suggest that ACs are unlikely to be homogeneous. As Jenkins (1989) pointed out the role of ACs will vary with factors like the size of the board, the degree of non-executive representation, and organisational structure and concluded that 'the functions of an audit committee must therefore be matched to the needs of the business concerned. No standard set of functions will do'. Other possible reasons for variations in the scope of ACs include: the wide age profile of ACs, the past experience of the instigators of ACs in the organisation; and evolutionary changes, which may occur

85

due to specific circumstances and different members being appointed to the AC.

Mautz and Neuman (1976) suggested that as ACs mature the range of functions assigned to them increase. Table 15 indicates that this was not always the case for the UK.

Table 15

Comparison of the age of an AC and the number of functions
assigned to the AC

	Number of functions			
	up to 9	10 to 19	20 and over	Total
Age in years				
up to 5	7	22	24	53
6 to 10	2	13	16	31
over 10	2	7	9	18
	11	42	49	102

Although the highest concentration of ACs with a low number of functions is found among recently formed ACs, the percentage of organisations whose AC had over 20 functions is not very different for recently formed ACs at 45% than for the other two age categories

86

(52% and 50% respectively) and statistically there is no association.[28] The probable reason for this is that, although older ACs evolve to cover an increased number of functions, many organisations setting up an AC for the first time seek to determine best practice and copy fully evolved AC models. Certainly many of the respondents talked to by the author were eager to discover the AC practices of other leading firms.

The range of functions covered by ACs was considerably greater than was reported by Chambers and Snook (1979) and Marrian (1988). In particular involvement with internal auditors and responsibility of internal control matters had increased. This wider range of functions suggests that the productivity of ACs has increased. Discussions with three respondents whose firms had ACs over five years old revealed that the responsibilities of ACs had gradually increased without more than a marginal rise in the meeting time. The resultant gap had been closed by factors like: the non-executive directors becoming more experienced; improved briefing papers; and more time devoted to preparation.

The importance of functions covered by ACs was measured in two ways. First, the percentage of respondents reporting each of the functions listed, and second, a rank. The rank was determined by asking respondents to rank what were considered to be the five most important functions carried out by the organisation's AC. The ranks were scored from 1 to 5 (most important to least important). The average score for each function was used to create a hierarchy of the functions of the 87 firms completing this section. The rank column in

---

[28] The null hypothesis of no association is accepted. Chi-squared value 1.0397 with 4 degrees of freedom compared to a critical value of 9.488 at the 95% confidence level.

Tables 16 to 19 reflects the importance of each function determined in this fashion.

Table 16

External reporting functions assigned to the AC

	% of respondents	Rank
External reporting		
Review company accounting principles and practice, and significant changes during the year	94	1
Review audited annual financial statements	91	2
Review interim reports	79	4
Review entire annual report	66	3
Monitor compliance with statutory and Stock Exchange reporting requirements	52	5
Review summary financial reports	47	6
Review circulars issued in respect of takeovers, defence against takeovers and other major non-routine transactions	38	8
Review prior to issue press statements and advertisements relating to financial matters	33	7

There was consistency between the number of ACs with a particular function and the ranking. In the organisations surveyed ACs were invariably responsible for the review of company accounting principles and practice and the review of audited annual financial statements. Reviewing interim reports and the entire annual report were also present among the functions of a significant number of respondents. The last four items in Table 16 will not be applicable to all the respondents, but as 90% of the organisations are UK based listed companies for whom such items are relevant, it is apparent that these functions are of lesser importance than the first four functions.

Table 17 shows strong agreement on the relative importance of the various functions as between the incidence of various functions and the ranking. The primary external audit functions are to discuss the audit with the external auditors, discuss the audited accounts and review the external auditors evaluation of internal controls. Carrying out these functions typically involved one or more meetings between the AC and the partner/partners responsible for the audit. There was invariably a meeting to review the annual financial statement and the auditor's report. It was uncommon for the AC to review the scope of external audit work prior to it commencing. Organisations also reported that a representative of the external auditors was normally at the board meeting when the annual accounts were approved and the AC final report considered. The review of the internal control systems allows AC members to obtain an independent opinion on the strength of the internal controls in the organisation and makes the executive accountable for implementing control recommendations. The power to review audit fees was not rated as being of any great importance but was nevertheless present in almost half of the respondents' ACs.' This function is obviously linked with the review of audit scope as increases in scope will increase fees. The ability to nominate auditors was a function in only a third of the ACs. Several organisations with the function stressed its importance as a means of ensuring auditor independence and the selection of the best, rather than the cheapest audit bid. In the two organisations where the matter was discussed the nomination of auditors was held to be a recently acquired function and

---

Table 17

External auditors' functions assigned to the AC

External auditors	% of respondents	Rank
Discuss with the auditors their experiences and problems in carrying out the audit	97	1
Discuss the meaning and significance of audited figures and notes attached thereto	95	2
Review their evaluation of the company's internal control systems, recommendations to management and management's response	93	3
Review factors that might impair, or be perceived to impair the auditor's independence	79	4
Discuss scope and timing of audit work	67	5
Review proposed audit fees	49	8
Arbitrate disputes between the auditors and management	47	6 =
Approve the auditors	44	9
Nominate the auditors	31	6 =

---

would always be ratified by the board. The function of arbitrating disputes was stated to be inapplicable or never to have arisen in a number of organisations. This reflects either the harmonious state of relationships between auditors and management in such

---

Table 18

Internal auditors functions assigned to the AC

Internal auditors	% of respondents	Rank
Discuss the effectiveness of internal controls	84	4 =
Review internal audit objectives and plans	82	3
Discuss with the internal auditors the findings and reports	80	2
Ascertain whether proper action has been taken on recommendations	80	4 =
Evaluate the adequacy of the resources devoted to internal audit	78	6
Review organisation of the department, lines of reporting and independence of the internal audit function	77	1
Discuss with the auditors their experience and problems in carrying out the audit	73	7
Discuss the relationship between internal and external auditors and the co-ordination of their audit work	69	8

organisations or an unwillingness to admit that disputes arise. Certainly, positive responses often included the caveat like 'if these ever arise' or 'a circumstance that has never arisen'.

Table 18 shows consistency in the range of functions carried out by ACs in the companies surveyed since the minimum occurrence of a function identified in the questionnaire was almost 70%. However, there is some difference between the ranking of functions and their occurrence. In particular, the review of the department and its' position within the organisation was highly rated in those organisations where it was a function but was the sixth most frequently occurring functions. A finance director stated that the independence and effectiveness of internal auditors was a key objective of the AC as their contribution to strong controls, effectiveness and fraud prevention was of more significance than that of the external auditors. Also for ACs where detailed discussion was limited, an overview of the organisation of the internal auditor department was deemed a useful way of spending the time available. Among the respondents with whom the matter was discussed the depth of the review of the internal auditors' findings and reports varied widely. In some organisations copies of all reports was tabled, while elsewhere a filtering process limited the review to summaries or selected items. The relationship between and the co-ordination of the work of internal and external auditors was ranked least important and appeared least frequently. The explanation most commonly received was that the matter was considered to be an operational matter in management's planning of the audit and therefore not a prime concern of the AC. The findings suggest a strong emphasis on internal controls and an effective internal audit function. Internal auditors, with whom discussions were held, all stressed that reporting to the AC enhanced their independence and status, and added weight to their recommendations. A further advantage to the firm is that exposure at board level motivates internal auditors to improve the quality of their reports since it is known that reports are seen by directors.

Table 19

Functions under the heading 'other matters' assigned to the AC

	% of respondents	Rank
Other matters		
Enquire into illegal, questionable, or unethical activities	66	1
Initiate special projects or investigations on any matter within its terms of reference	53	3
Monitor adherence of officials to the corporate code of conduct	40	2
Review significant transactions outside the company's normal business	32	5
Review the adequacy of management information systems	24	6
Ensure the board receives reliable and timely management information	20	4
Review the efforts of the company to comply with social obligations to the employees, the community and others	8	7

As is shown in Table 19 only two functions are widespread. The remainder vary from adherence to the corporate code of conduct, which appears in 40% of the ACs, to reviewing compliance with social obligations, which was only reported by eight organisations. The rankings vary to an extent with the frequency with which ACs have the functions; although there is agreement on first and last position. The main contradiction, the function of ensuring that the board receives reliable and timely management information, was explicitly recognised in only a fifth of respondents but where it was mentioned it was among the ranked items.

Respondents were also asked to indicate whether there were any additional functions under the headings (external reporting; external audit; internal audit; and other matters) which were not among the 32 functions listed. None were mentioned beyond the following items under other matters:

review the terms of reference of the AC (three instances);

receive the minutes or reports from subsidiary ACs (five instances);

receive reports on substantial frauds or other losses occasioned by a lack of internal control;

review insurance cover periodically;

enquire about the situation on major law suits (two instances);

review transactions between the company and board members* (three instances);

review the expenses of board members* (two instances);

review the policies and procedures for ratifying senior executives pay*;

review conflict of interest procedures*;

94

monitor security matters;

review contract audit procedures;
capital expenditure approval, investment appraisal and post implementation audit on major items (three instances)**;

review value for money initiatives; and

consider other matters which the AC is invited by the board to review.

the responsibility of the remuneration of committee in a number of organisations*.

Chambers and Snook (1979) found that a quarter of ACs had a responsibility for finance and expenditure matters like reviewing the finance and expenditure plans of the group and considering proposals on financial targets and major capital expenditure items. These finance type functions result from ACs evolving from finance committees and apart from these examples ACs no longer appear to have these responsibilities**.

One company reported that their AC structure was not a derivative of US practice but rather an integral part of corporate control mechanisms over a diversified group. The AC structure involves a group AC and sub ACs in the various businesses. The group AC comprises mainly non-executive directors (finance director, director of control, two non-executive directors and one other board member) but in sub ACs the criterion is directors with the widest spread of control. The ACs are responsible for ensuring that there are appropriate controls throughout the group and, in particular, the ACs are charged with:

identifying the key controls for each business;

95

examining the scope of control activity internally and externally;

determining the scope of the work of the internal and external auditors and the extent to which their work addresses the key control issues on which the business depends; and

deciding on the weight to be given to various control activity cycles.

The work of the ACs involves not only the present control environment but also a review of likely changes in management and decision-making systems in the medium to longer term and their implications for key controls in businesses. Further, the AC was also more productive in its involvement with auditors. The AC is responsible for the choice of external auditors. The selection is based on an assessment of the quality of the assignment partners at each of the locations, the scope of the audit and the potential value added by the work. The AC system also has a key role in monitoring compliance with ethical standards. The group standards are clear but ethics is a comparative issue, which must take some account of local conditions. The local AC can adapt the standards but must report back to the group AC so that the board can sign off on ethical issues. The approach replaced the old hierarchical control system for a model where responsibility for control is vested locally with the ACs acting to maintain an appropriate control environment and identify and report potential control problems.

Factors affecting the effectiveness of ACs

In discussions with the author, respondents with an AC consistently felt that the AC fulfilled a useful function and were intending to continue with an AC. The questionnaire sought to discover whether there is any agreement on which attributes contribute to AC success.

Respondents were asked to indicate the extent to which they agreed that certain attributes of AC members are very important using a scale from 1 signifying strongly agree to 5 signifying strongly disagree. Table 20 shows the mean and standard deviation (std dev) of the responses.

Table 20

Opinions on the importance of attributes of AC members in contributing to the success of ACs

	Mean	Std dev
Sound judgement	1.33	0.57
Independence from management	1.42	0.64
Full understanding of purposes and responsibilities of the audit committee	1.43	0.70
Enthusiastic chairman	1.58	0.78
Variety of backgrounds among the committee members	1.68	0.86
Ability to devote the necessary time	1.76	0.74
Knowledge of company's business areas	2.00	0.82
Knowledge of finance, accounting and auditing	2.15	0.99

As might be anticipated, given the nature of the statements, there was broad agreement that the attributes were important since all the attributes had a mean below the scale mean of three. In fact, only five instances of respondents strongly disagreeing with any attributes occurred and only 30 instances of 'disagree somewhat' were reported. Nevertheless, the summarised responses reveal that certain attributes in the list are considered to be more important than others. Sound judgement, independence and a clear awareness of the role of the AC were deemed by respondents to be more important than knowledge either of the business or of finance, accounting and auditing. Indeed, over 65% of respondents strongly agree that these attributes of AC members are very important in contributing to the success of ACs and only 27% and 23% respectively strongly agree with the importance of knowledge of the companies business areas or knowledge of finance, accounting and auditing. A respondent stated that relevant briefing and advice was always available to AC members and that the important quality that AC members brought to the proceedings was experience of different environments and an ability to question the reasons or decisions. However, most non-executive directors, although not specialists in accounting or auditing, would have a wide enough business experience to ask relevant questions and evaluate answers. Another respondent commented that it was the mix of skills on the AC that was important. This was supported by disclosure of AC membership in the accounts, which showed that there was often at least one qualified accountant on the AC.

Respondents suggested that the following attributes, not included in the questionnaire, were very important:

personal qualities like common sense, probing approach, firmness, tenacity, integrity and an ability to identify and focus upon the fundamental issues;

experience at board level across a number of different businesses and functions;

a willingness to take the AC seriously; and

experience of working practices in a number of different countries.

Respondents were asked to indicate the extent to which they agree that various practices are very important in contributing to the success of the AC. Again, a scale from 1 signifying strongly agree to 5 signifying strongly disagree was used. Table 21 shows the mean and standard deviation (std dev) of the responses.

The results show broad agreement with the practices being very important for successful ACs with all but three practices scoring below two against a scale mean of three. Even the item rotation of membership, which was rated lowest, had only 49% of respondents disagreeing. In contrast, the first four practices in the Table had over or just below 65% of respondents stating that they strongly agreed. Respondents stated that many of the practices were already in place in the organisation. The conflict between the lack of support for both continuity of membership and rotation of membership needs explanation. The lack of importance of rotation of membership is consistent with the prior finding that appointments to the AC are normally for an indefinite term. However, continuity of memberships, although common, is not deemed to be a very important practice for a successful AC. Occasional changes in membership were not viewed as detrimental but regular changes would prevent expertise being developed and could be disruptive and impractical given the small pool of non-executive directors available to many firms.

Additional practices, which were considered very important by respondents included:

regular meetings and the ability to call additional meetings as necessary;

attendance of non-members as required eg. finance director; external audit partner or head of internal audit;

Table 21

Importance of various factors in contributing to the success of ACs

	Mean	Std dev
Availability of relevant information	1.23	0.45
Provision of an agenda and related material in advance of meetings	1.37	0.56
Ready access to external auditors	1.40	0.62
Ready access to internal auditors	1.54	0.70
Prompt answering of queries	1.71	0.79
Written statement of objectives and responsibilities	1.85	0.88
Prompt notification of problems by management	1.92	0.92
Careful selection of members	1.96	0.89
Continuity of membership	2.01	0.79
Independence from the main board	2.02	1.26
Rotation of membership	3.40	0.99

written AC objectives; and

senior management support and ready access to all levels of management.

A question sought to obtain the opinions of respondents on three statements using the scale from 1 signifying strongly agree to 5 indicating strongly disagree. The mean and standard deviation (std dev) of the responses are contained in Table 22.

Table 22

Opinions on key issues

	Mean	Std dev
Companies with a Stock Exchange quotation should be required by law to have an audit committee	2.11	1.20
The audit committee should be allowed to use internal audit staff to assist the committee members to discharge their responsibilities	2.34	1.31
The audit committee should be allowed to engage outside technical specialists to assist the committee members to discharge their responsibilities	2.91	1.33

The results, with the responses mean all being below the scale mean of 3, suggest that there are varying degrees of support for the AC having the powers in the statements or being required by law. There was general acceptance of the first statement since it was strongly agreed with by 40% of respondents, agreed with to an extent by 30% of respondents and only 20% of respondents indicated any degree of disagreement. Perhaps the results for a legal requirement reflect some of the ambivalence expressed by Lord Bancroft in the 1988 debate in the House of Lords: 'None of the speakers in the House of Lords debate objected to audit committees in principle. In fact, most supported them. What they objected to was use of the law'.[29] Reasons put forward for agreeing with a legal requirement largely centred on improving corporate governance and hence overall confidence in the sector. Some respondents also stated that it was the only way to get the companies that most needed ACs to form them. Reasons for disagreeing with a legal requirement for ACs included that an AC can only be effective with the full support of the board and management; and that an enforced AC may well be seen as a bureaucratic imposition to which only 'lip service' would be paid. Alternatively, if ACs are as effective as is claimed, their advantages should be self-evident, in which case legal imposition is unnecessary. The results show a shift in opinion since the survey by Marrian (1988), which reported that 'the majority of interviewees were against making audit committees mandatory for listed companies'. The use of internal audit to assist the AC members in discharging their responsibilities was generally accepted by the majority. There was agreement to some extent by 67% of respondents and disagreement to an extent by only 18% of respondents. Some respondents stated that this effectively already happened due to regular meetings with and questioning of the head of internal audit. A greater divergence of opinion emerged over the proposition of allowing ACs to engage outside specialists: 47% agreed to an extent but 33% disagreed with 18% strongly disagreeing.

---

[29] As quoted in Jenkins, B. (1989), 'Audit Committees: Where Now?' Managerial Auditing Journal, Vol. 4, pp. 14-16.

Disclosure of the information about the AC in the annual report and accounts

The Accountants International Study Group (1977) recommended that 'the annual report of a corporation indicate the existence of an audit committee and identify its members'. However, the disclosure of information on ACs is voluntary in the UK. Nevertheless, 66 organisations with an AC (65%) disclosed some information on the AC in the annual report and accounts. This is an increase on the 50% level of disclosure reported by Marrian (1988).

Three levels of disclosure about an AC were identified in the questionnaire: existence; objectives and functions; and members. Combinations of these levels were: at a minimum only the existence of an AC was disclosed; above this level the existence and membership were disclosed; and finally the existence, membership and objectives and functions were all disclosed. Table 23 shows the extent of disclosure reported by respondents.

The results reveal that the commonest disclosure, which was followed by 47% of respondents, is a combination of the existence of an AC and the membership. The disclosure was normally made in a section of the annual report and accounts with a heading like: 'Directors'; 'The Board'; or 'Management Structure'. Although in a minority of cases, information was given in the Report of the Directors. Information on the membership of the AC was given in the following ways:

a list of the members of the AC;
a reference to AC membership in the biographical details of directors;
an annotation on a list of directors; and
a statement that all non-executive directors were members of the AC.

Table 23

Disclosure of AC in the annual report and accounts

	Number of respondents	% of respondents disclosing data
The existence of an AC only	6	9
The existence of an AC and the identity of audit committee members	48	73
Full disclosure	12	18
	66	100

The fuller disclosure varied in detail and position. In the case of the Grand Metropolitan PLC Annual Report 1990, a section 'Board of Directors' contained the following detailed disclosure:

GrandMet Board Committees

Audit: consisting of non-executive directors only, but with the internal and external auditors, Chairman & Chief Executive, Group Finance Director and Group Financial Controller normally in attendance. Meets at least three times a year to consider audit, accountancy and financial control matters and to ensure appropriate procedures are in place.

In addition there was also a separate page devoted to 'Corporate Governance', which also alluded to the role of the AC.

While, Reckitt & Coleman PLC in the 1991 Annual Report provided similar, but perhaps more comprehensive, information under a section headed 'Committees of the board'.

Audit Committee

The audit committee, which was established in 1978 provides a link between the board and the company's auditors on matters coming within the scope of the group audit. Those matters include accounting standards and policies generally, internal financial control procedures and the group accounts and reports which are intended for publication. The committee, which comprises all of the non-executive directors of the company under the chairmanship of Mr M R Valentine, meets regularly before the publication of the group's interim and preliminary year-end results and at other times as required. It does not involve itself in the day to day running of the business which remains the responsibility of the executive directors.

An example of information on ACs provided in the Directors Report was given by George Wimpey PLC in the 1991 Annual Report, which disclosed:

Audit Committee

The Audit Committee consists of three non-executive directors: Mr W P C Grassick (Chairman), Dr D J T Graves and Mr P A M Curry. The objects of the committee are to review the effectiveness of both internal and external audit, financial controls and internal checks, to consider major accounting issues and developments and to review the annual report and accounts.

The most succinct disclosure was the reference by IMI plc in the 1990 Annual Report in the 'Board of Directors' section, which limited the role of the AC to matters related to the accounts by stating:

> There are two Committees of the Board consisting of the Non-Executive Directors: a Salaries and Appointments Committee determines the remuneration of Executive Directors and an Audit Committee, established in 1977, considers with the auditors matters relating to accounts.

However, in general despite the above exceptions, information on the AC in respondents annual accounts was not easy to find. This supports the views held by respondent's with whom the matter was discussed which include: annual accounts are already overcrowded; the fuss about corporate governance will die down and it is not worth pandering to a passing fashion; the existence of an AC is an internal matter; the existence of an AC is of little consequence to the users of accounts (one finance director stated 'the average non-institutional shareholder would be unlikely to know the effect of having an AC'); and the existence of an AC would be presumed by users. Two respondents indicated that disclosure of information on the AC had never been considered. The opinion was also expressed that if the existence and nature of an AC is specifically disclosed then a full breakdown of the committee structure of the board and the company's corporate governance philosophy should be given. Certainly the examples of Grand Metropolitan plc, Reckitt & Coleman plc and IMI plc revealed some movement in this direction.

Summary

The results of the questionnaire show the following:

The number of organisations with ACs

Of the 250 major industrial concerns that were identified as the top 250 organisations in the Times 1000 1989-1990, 80% responded to the questionnaire. Of these 53% had an AC, which included amongst its' members at least one non-executive director. ACs were most frequent among the largest firms. Public sector organisations and recently privatised companies invariably had ACs. ACs were present in two-thirds of UK listed companies but were infrequent in subsidiaries of foreign corporations and unquoted organisations.

ACs appear to be a relatively new phenomenon since the majority were established since 1986 and over 80% established since 1980.

Of the 102 respondents with an AC, 19 reported that there are other ACs (usually below three and situated outside the UK) within the group. In just over half of these instances there are links between the main AC and subsidiary ACs; usually through the minutes of reports being submitted to the main AC.

The reasons given by respondents for not having an AC stressed the additional bureaucracy involved and the failure of the anticipated benefits to outweigh the costs. ACs were also seen as inappropriate to foreign subsidiaries, unquoted companies and companies with relatively small boards. A number of respondents stated that the main reason for not having an AC was that existing arrangements for board/auditor communications were satisfactory.

The motives for having an AC

The strongest motive reported was good corporate practice. Other important motives were: strengthening the role and effectiveness of non-executive directors; assisting the directors in discharging their statutory responsibilities as regards financial reporting; enhancing the independence of internal and external auditors; and improving communications between the board and internal and external auditors.

AC practices and procedures

Half of the respondents had an AC composed solely of non-executive directors. The number of members on an AC varied from two to eleven but the norm was three or four members. Typically, appointments were made by the board, by a committee of the board or were automatic because all non-executive directors were on the board. Appointments were for an indefinite period in 82% of cases. There were no bars to membership of the AC apart from being an executive director.

The ACs of respondents met two or three times per year on a regular basis for a period of around two hours. The total average annual time spent on AC meetings is 6.5 hours but there was considerable difference between different types of organisation with UK listed companies averaging 8.2 hours compared with 5.8 hours for the rest. The duties and responsibilities of ACs are usually specified in written terms of reference, board resolutions or both. Minutes are prepared for all AC meetings. The minutes are widely distributed and are certainly received by AC members and the main board.

Functions assigned to ACs

ACs carry out a wide range of functions involving external reporting, external auditors, internal auditors and other matters. On average respondents had 18 of the 32 functions listed in the questionnaire under these four categories. The functions relating to external reporting, which were present in over 75% of respondents in order of the frequency of occurrence were:

(i) review company accounting principles and practices, and significant changes during the year

(ii) review audited annual financial statements

(iii) review interim report

The functions related to external auditors, which were present in over 75% of respondents in order of the frequency of occurrence were:

(i) discuss with the auditors their experiences and problems in carrying out the audit

(ii) discuss the meaning and significance of audited figures and notes attached thereto

(iii) review their evaluation of the company's internal control systems, recommendations to management and management's response

(iv) review factors that might impair, or be perceived to impair the auditor's independence

The AC approves appointment of the auditors for 44% of respondents and only 31% reported that the AC nominates the auditors.

The functions related to internal auditors, which were present in over 75% of respondents in order of the frequency of occurrence were:

(i) discuss the effectiveness of internal controls

(ii)   review internal audit objectives and plans

(iii) discuss with the internal auditors their findings and reports

(iv) ascertain whether proper action has been taken on recommendations

 (v) evaluate the adequacy of the resources devoted to internal audit

(vi) review organisation of the department, lines of reporting and independence of the internal audit function

(vii) discuss with the auditors their experiences and problems in carrying out the audit.

Of the functions under the heading 'other matters', none were present in the functions of the ACs of over 75% of respondents and only the following were present in the functions of the ACs of over 50% of respondents:

(i)   enquire into illegal, questionable or unethical activities

(ii)   initiate special projects or investigations on any matter within its terms of reference.

Effectiveness of ACs

The most important attributes of AC members for a successful AC were judged by the respondents to be:

(i)   sound judgement

(ii)   independence from management

(iii) full understanding of purposes and responsibilities of the audit committee

(iv) enthusiastic chairman

A knowledge of the company's business areas and a knowledge of finance, accounting and auditing were not deemed by respondents to be important attributes for AC members.

The factors, which were considered by respondents to be most important in contributing to the success of ACs, were:

(i) availability of relevant information

(ii) provision of an agenda and related material in advance of meetings

(iii) ready access to external and internal auditors

(iv) prompt answering of queries

Unsurprisingly given that appointments to the AC are usually for an indefinite term, little importance was given to rotation of membership.

Respondents showed some enthusiasm for propositions that ACs should be required by law for companies with a stock exchange quotation and that ACs should be allowed to use internal audit staff to discharge their activities but there was a range of opinions on whether the latter proposition should be extended to permitting ACs to hire outside technical specialists.

Disclosure of an AC in the annual report and accounts

65% of respondents with ACs recorded some information on their AC in the annual report. The commonest form of disclosure, 73% of cases, was to record the existence of an AC and the membership. However in 18% of the annual reports the disclosure was extended to include information on the objectives and functions of the AC. Disclosure was generally either in a 'Directors' or 'Board' or 'Management Structure' section or in the Report of Directors. In general, information on the AC was not prominent and there was a belief that the existence or absence of such a committee was not of prime interest to the users of financial information.

Chapter 6

Audit Committees in Financial Institutions

The number of financial institutions with an AC

Full responses were received from 42 financial institutions. In addition, one financial institution refused to participate and another provided incomplete information. Both these financial institutions had an AC. This gave an overall response rate of 88% and a useable response rate of 84%. Table 1 analyses the total responses into financial institutions with an AC and financial institutions without an AC and details response rates.

The results suggest that UK listed financial institutions almost invariably have an AC. It is also probable that subsidiaries of foreign banks and other organisations will have an AC. An AC was present in all the clearing banks, insurance companies and building societies circularised. The large proportion of financial institutions with an AC reflects legislative and institutional pressure. Although an AC is not required by The Banking Act 1987, there is pressure for the appointment of non-executive directors and the formation of ACs. Sch.3, para. 3 requires authorised institutions to include an appropriate number (which could be none) of directors without executive responsibilities on the board and the Bank of England is required to have regard of the functions and responsibilities of non-executive directors when it is determining whether the systems of control are adequate. Further, The Financial Services Act 1986 could well lead to the formation of ACs, as a means of monitoring compliance. Institutional pressure arises from the commitment of the Bank of England to the principle that all banks and banking groups should have an AC. A position stated in a consultative paper (Bank of England, 1987).

113

Table 1

Number of financial institutions with an AC

Type of financial institution	With an AC	No AC	% of replies with an AC
Clearing banks (London and Scottish)	7	–	100
Other British banks	17	9	65
Insurance companies	6	–	100
Building societies	5	–	100
Total	35	9	88%

Status of financial institutions	With an AC	No AC	% of replies with an AC
UK based listed companies	23	1	96
Subsidiaries of a foreign bank	4	5	44
Public body	1	–	100
Other organisations	7	3	70
Total	35	9	88%

Those financial institutions without an AC fell into two groups: four financial institutions, which had no AC or body fulfilling the functions of an AC; and five financial institutions with a 'quasi AC'.

The four financial institutions without an AC comprise:

a UK listed company – the decision of this company not to have an AC was based on the reasons that an AC involves additional bureaucracy, that the costs of an AC exceed the benefits, and that there is no legal requirement to have an AC;

a subsidiary of a foreign bank– the absence of an AC was explained largely on the grounds that ACs act as a barrier between the auditor and the main board; and

two 'other organisations'– both private limited companies, one stated that ACs are mainly relevant to plcs, while the other reasons as follows: 'We only have three shareholders, all of whom are represented on the board and who therefore feel they do not need the protection of an audit committee.'

The five 'quasi ACs' were present in one 'other organisation' and four subsidiaries of foreign banks. The nature of the 'quasi ACs' were as follows:

the other organisation was an unlisted plc. The absence of a formal AC was countered by 'the board of *** sits as an audit committee from time to time under the chairmanship of one of the non-executive directors'. The company also stated that it was 'supportive of the general practice of major companies having audit committees or adopting similar practices'.

the most focused example of a 'quasi AC' was an AC at the subsidiary of a foreign bank, which was composed of three

115

sectional heads (administration, accounts and computing). The AC was responsible for following up recommendations of the head office internal auditors and the external auditors and also for progressing identified improvements. The approach was to convert auditors' recommendations into a list of actionable projects with the objective of reducing, if not eliminating, the number of items raised by the audit report. It was reported that the approach has proved very successful.

The most active 'quasi AC' at the subsidiary of a foreign bank consisted of five executive directors (including the Group Audit Director, the Chairman of Bank and the Group Finance Director) and two non-executives (including Head of Internal Audit) and the external audit partner. The committee has ten regular meetings and two special meetings a year lasting, in total, almost 20 hours. The committee covers the review of annual financial statements, the review of interim reports, discussions with the external auditors about their experiences and problems in carrying out the audit, and discussions with the internal auditors about their findings and whether their recommendations have been properly actioned.

One subsidiary of a foreign parent liaised with the parent through an officer of the parent being the only non-executive member on the AC of four members including the Chairman and the Vice Chairman. The main tasks of the AC, which meets only twice a year, are to monitor compliance with statutory and Stock Exchange reporting requirements, review company accounting principles and practice, review the Bank of England prudential returns, discuss with the external auditors their audit findings and discuss the relationship between internal and external auditors.

The final 'quasi AC' in the subsidiary of a foreign bank was closest to the norm for ACs. The AC was composed of four directors and met four times a year usually for an hour. The AC considers a wide range of matters including reviewing of financial reports, discussing the findings of internal and external auditors, monitoring compliance with statutory and Stock Exchange requirements, reviewing of significant transactions, enquiring into fraud and illegal acts and initiating investigations.

The rest of this section and subsequent sections of the chapter focus on the responses of the 33 financial institutions with ACs (35 responses less the refusal and an incomplete response). The incomplete response was from the public sector body which, although it had an AC indicated that the workings of the AC would not be indicative. The AC scrutinises the end of year accounts and receives reports from internal and external auditors but it does not have an on-going monitoring role throughout the year.

Information on the age of the AC was provided by 32 respondents. The age distribution of the ACs surveyed is shown in Table 2.

ACs appear to be a relatively new phenomenon in financial institutions, with almost two-thirds being established in the last five years before January 1991. However, none were less than two years old. There are some long established ACs with four institutions reporting that the AC was over 20 years old. Interestingly of these four, two, a disproportionate number, were building societies. It was also noted that the ACs of the six insurance companies were all five years old or less, with an average of only three and a half years. Otherwise, each of the types of financial institutions had examples of all ages of AC. For instance, the age of ACs in the clearing banks ranged from over 20 years to three years.

Of respondents with an AC, 55% reported that there were other ACs in the group. Table 3 analyses the existence of multiple ACs by type

117

of financial institution, indicating whether or not the ACs are inter-related.

Table 2

Age of ACs

Years	Number of respondents	% of respondents
0-2	3	9
3-5	17	53
6-8	2	6
9-11	1	3
12-14	3	9
15 and over	6	20
	32	100

Multiple ACs were most frequent in clearing banks and insurance companies. Amongst other British banks the four respondents with ACs comprised: a subsidiary of a foreign bank, an unlisted financial institution and two UK listed financial institutions. The additional ACs operate in a range of institutions including: merchant banks; joint ventures; investment banks; major UK subsidiaries; and major overseas subsidiaries. One financial institution reported the existence of an AC for each of three operating divisions.

Table 3

Incidence of Multiple ACs

	Number with multiple ACs	%	Average	Maximum number of ACs	Minimum number of ACs
Clearing banks (London and Scottish)	6	86	4.0	9	1
Other British banks	4	25	2.0	3	1
Insurance companies	5	83	2.4	4	1
Building societies	3	60	1.3	2	1
Total	18	55%	2.8		

In 12 cases (67%) there was a link between the main AC and other ACs in the group. Table 4 analyses the method or methods by which this was achieved. The commonest methods were common/cross membership and the communication of the deliberations of subsidiary ACs through a written report or minutes presented to the main AC. A variety of different common members were reported including: a finance director and two non-executive directors; a chief finance officer; a group chief internal auditor; and the divisional AC chairman. The institutions without links gave reasons like: the lack of materiality of the unit with an AC; and internal audit under head office control and identical external auditors (the implication being that problems at subsidiaries would be reported to the head office AC).

Table 4

Method of inter-relationship between ACs

	Number of financial institutions
Common/cross membership of ACs	6
Minutes/reports sent to head office AC or a member thereof	8
Common charter/Terms of Reference	1

Note: some financial institutions reported that more than one method was used.

The motives for having an AC

Respondents were asked to indicate on a scale from 1 (strongly agree) to 5 (strongly disagree) the extent to which they agreed that each of 13 motives reflects a reason for having an AC in the organisation. Table 5 lists the 13 reasons in order of the extent of agreement as determined by the mean score of responses. Information on the standard deviation (std dev) is given to indicate the relative dispersion of the responses.

'Good corporate practice' was clearly the dominant motive with 73% strongly agreeing. As one finance director says 'the idea of audit committees being established as a sensible method of delegating the financial reporting and control responsibilities of the directors is now well established'. One respondent opined that the increasing financial reporting requirements, the new regulatory environment, growth in the

Table 5

Motives for having an AC

Motives		Mean	Std dev
1.	good corporate practice	1.30	0.53
2.	assists directors in discharging their statutory responsibilities as regards financial reporting	1.79	0.65
3.	preserves and enhances the independence of internal auditors	1.91	1.07
4.	improves communications between the board and internal auditors	1.94	0.97
5.	strengthens the role and effectiveness of non-executive directors	2.00	0.97
6.	improves communications between the board and external auditors	2.15	0.76
7.	assists management to discharge its responsibilities for the prevention of fraud, other irregularities and errors	2.27	1.10
8 = .	preserves and enhances the independence of external auditors	2.49	1.25
8 = .	assists the auditors in the reporting of serious deficiencies in the control environment or management weaknesses	2.49	1.25
10.	possibility of legislative pressure	2.82	1.42
11.	increases the confidence of the public in the credibility and objectivity of financial statements	3.39	1.20
12.	provides a forum for arbitration between management and auditors	3.39	1.20
13.	increases the confidence of investment analysts in the credibility and objectivity of financial statements	3.42	0.94

size and spread of activities of financial organisations and the complexity of control systems had all contributed to the formation of ACs. The motive with the next highest 'strongly agree' rating was 'preserves and enhances the independence of internal auditors' (42%), followed by 'improves communications between the board and external auditors' (39%) and 'strengthens the role and effectiveness of non-executive directors (36%).

In discussions with the author two respondents suggested that internal auditors have a crucial role to play in vetting control systems and uncovering corrupt and fraudulent activities. The stress on internal auditors rather than external auditors, it was suggested, reflects the limited ability of the latter to uncover fraud and corrupt practices in financial institutions. The motive 'assists directors in discharging their statutory responsibilities as regards financial reporting', although second on mean score, had the strong agreement of only 33% of respondents.

As might have been expected, since the list of motives given were deliberately plausible, all but three of the motives had a mean below the scale average of three. The motives were those relating to public confidence in financial statements; provision of a forum for arbitration; and the confidence of investment analysts. The lack of aversion to even these motives is indicated by percentage of respondents strongly disagreeing, ranging from only 12% to 24%. The highest level of disagreement was against the motive 'provides a forum for arbitration between management and auditors'. This could well be explained by the unwillingness of some respondents to accept that such disputes could arise.

Respondents were asked to indicate whether there were any other motives, which could lead to the establishment of an AC. The most frequently mentioned motives include:

'assists the directors in discharging their responsibilities as regards regulatory compliance'. This was reported by three of the banks. Discussions with other financial institutions suggested that in some cases, this responsibility was carried out by a separate compliance committee.[30] One building society stated that a motive for forming an AC was advice from the regulatory body.

'improves the effectiveness of internal auditors'. This was suggested by four respondents. ACs were seen to enhance the status of internal auditors and emphasise the importance of internal auditors and their responsibilities.

'wider forum for the discussion of accounting matters' or 'lack of board time for detail'. These were motives for three respondents. Increased complexity in accounting and the widening scope of financial reporting mean that a company's board of directors has difficulty in giving sufficient time for a detailed discussion of these matters. The AC provides the ideal forum.

'board policy' and 'becoming common city practice'. These were also mentioned. The latter suggests a feeling, as stated by one chief financial officer, that ACs are an evolutionary response to the increasing demands on the board, due to the changes over the last few years in the control, financial reporting and regulatory environments.

---

[30] Peat Marwick McLintock (1987) refer to such committees as follows: 'Although there is no specific reference to audit committees in the draft SIB Conduct of Business Rules or draft SRO regulations, the audit committee may well emerge in many cases as the means of monitoring compliance within investment business and might be called 'the audit and compliance committee'. In other cases, investment businesses may create a separate compliance committee of the board.'

AC practices and procedures

The questionnaire sought to determine the membership of audit committees: 22 financial institutions (67%) had an AC composed solely of non-executive directors; two financial institutions (6%) had non-executive directors and other members on the AC; five financial institutions (15%) had executive and non-executive directors on the AC; and four (12%) had an AC comprising all three categories of members. The maximum number of members of an AC was seven (three executive directors and four non-executive directors) and the minimum number was two (both non-executive directors). Table 6 shows the distribution of membership of the respondents' ACs analysed by the categories established. In examining the figures, it must be remembered that in some organisations the finance director and/or representatives of the external auditors and/or the head of internal audit were members of the AC, whereas in other organisations, they

Table 6

Number of members of ACs

	0	1-2	3-4	5-6	7-8	Mean	Std dev
Executive director	24	8	1	–	–	0.39	0.79
Non-executive directors	–	4	23	6	–	3.49	1.00
Other members	27	6	–	–	–	0.21	0.49
Total membership	–	1	22	8	1	4.09	1.16

were not members but merely in attendance. The responses suggest that the typical AC is composed of three or four non-executive directors.

The executive directors typically include the finance director but also mentioned, amongst others, were: the chairman, the chief executive, the deputy chairman, the deputy chief executive and chairman of the compliance committee. Other members were normally the external audit partner/s but others specified included: a representative of the holding company; the Head of Group Internal Audit; an independent full time consultant; and the group compliance officer.

Table 7

Normal term of the appointment of a director of the AC

	Number of respondents	% of responses
One year	1	3
Two years	1	3
Three years	3	9
Indefinite	28	85
	33	100

Table 7 shows that directors are normally appointed to the AC for an indefinite term. One explanation for this is that non-executive directors with an interest in the area are not numerous enough to permit rotation. An indefinite term of membership also has the advantage of allowing members to develop expertise and an awareness of the likely contentious areas. As one company secretary stated, 'the AC benefits from continuity of membership as it reduces the preparation for and discussion on current issues which have arisen in previous years'. However, it could be argued that indefinite membership breeds complacency and stifles innovative approaches. Members also become bound by the precedent created by past decisions in which they have been involved.

Table 8

Selection of AC members

| | Number of respondents | |
	Executive directors	Non-executive directors
By all the board	6	21
By the AC chairperson	2	7
By the board and chairperson	–	2
By a committee of the board	–	1
By the parent company	–	1
By board and AC chairpersons	1	1
	9	33

Table 8 shows that in the majority of cases, both executive director members (67%) and non-executive director members (64%) of the AC were selected by the board.

In all but one instance the appointments to the AC were ratified by the board. However, in an exceptional case the appointments made by the chairperson of a building society AC were not subject to the approval of the board.

Table 9

Conditions debarring a board member from serving on the AC

	Number of respondents
Holding a substantial amount of shares or loan stock in the company	1
Holding some shares or loan stock in the company	1
Holding a specific office	6
Being an executive director	24
A lack of financial, accounting or audit knowledge	5
No bars	4

Table 9 reveals that the main bar to a board member serving on an AC is being an executive director. This reflects the policy, in the majority of financial institutions with ACs, of limiting membership of the AC to non-executive directors. The debarring of persons with a specific office from membership of the AC relates to limitations, in financial institutions where this is permitted, on either which executive directors may be members or a bar on the chairperson being a member. The failure to debar from service board members, with shares or stock in the financial institution, is to be anticipated in such large institutions, as it is unlikely that any individual will have a material holding.

Only 15% of respondents felt that a lack of financial, accounting or audit knowledge was a bar to a board member serving on an AC. It was generally agreed that an executive or non-executive director would have a broad knowledge auditing and controls and that what was required was a breath of knowledge of such matters rather than technical depth.

Of respondents with an AC, 79% reported that the chairperson of the AC is selected by the board. Variations in the method for selecting the AC chairperson included: by the AC with ratification by the board; chairperson's recommendation with ratification by the board; by the non-executive directors; and the board chairperson is ex officio chairperson of the AC.

The AC secretary is the company secretary, assistant company secretary or nominee of the company secretary in 76% of respondents with an AC. Others reported as holding the post by more than one respondent are: the finance director (two instances) and the head of internal audit (two instances).

The frequency of AC meetings does not vary greatly. The majority of respondents (82%) reported that their ACs only hold regular meetings. Amongst the reasons given for special meetings were: to review defence or takeover documents; and to consider a revised corporate code of conduct. Table 10 shows the frequency of annual AC meetings analysed into four categories.

Table 10

Frequency of AC meetings each year

	0	1-2	3-4	over 4	Mean	Std dev
				Number		
Regular meetings	–	4	26	3	3.58	0.83
Special meetings	27	6	–	–	0.27	0.63
Total annual meetings	–	4	23	6	3.85	1.18

The most commonly occurring number of meetings is four, which is reported by 16 respondents (48%). The meetings are typically held quarterly. The maximum number of meetings is six with the maximum number of regular meetings being five and the maximum number of special meetings being two.

The average duration of meetings shows little variation amongst respondents. The maximum average duration reported is three hours and the minimum half an hour. Regular meetings have a mean average duration of two hours and special meetings have a mean average duration of 1.25 hours.

The shortest annual average duration of AC meetings is two hours (two meetings of one hour each) reported by an 'other British bank' and the longest is 15 hours (five meetings of three hours) at a building society. The overall mean annual average duration is 7.4 hours but there is considerable difference between building societies (mean 11.7 hours) and the other groups (mean 6.5 hours). It was pointed out by respondents in discussions with the author that meeting time is partly a function of the time spent on preparation and the quality of the briefing papers. Therefore, a short formal meeting does not necessarily equate with the tasks of the AC being performed in a cursory fashion.

The duties and functions of all but one of the ACs are formally stated. Table 11 shows how the duties and responsibilities were specified.

Of respondent financial institutions with ACs, 70% have the duties and responsibilities of the AC formalised by written terms of reference (see Appendix 3 for an example). In four of these instances the duties and responsibilities of the AC were also given in a separate charter. A further nine received their duties and responsibilities from board resolutions; in one case, supplemented by a separate charter. From a review of four examples of board resolutions and written terms of reference, the board resolutions appear to be much less detailed and specific than the written terms of reference.

Minutes were produced for AC meetings by all the respondents. The minutes were widely distributed as is illustrated in Table 12. It appears to be common for minutes to be distributed to members of the AC, members of the board, internal auditors and external auditors. The minutes distributed to the board were an important means of communicating the deliberations of the AC to the board. In one instance where this did not occur, the AC chairman made an oral report to the full board, which was minuted.

130

Table 11

Specification of the duties and responsibilities of the ACs

	Number of respondents
Board resolutions	8
Board resolutions and a separate charter	1
Written terms of reference	10
Written terms of reference and board resolutions*	9
Board resolutions, a separate charter and written terms of reference	4
An informal agreement	1
	33

*   includes a respondent with the duties and responsibilities also specified in a high level control manual.

Table 12

Distribution of minutes

	Number of respondents	% of respondents
Members of the committee	30	94
Board members	28	88
External auditors	24	75
Internal auditors	20	62
Senior management	10	31
Those in attendance	24	75

Note: One respondent did not give any details

Functions assigned to ACs

Respondents were asked to indicate which of 32 possible functions–
analysed into the categories: external reporting; external auditors;
internal auditors; and other matters – were assigned to ACs in their
organisation. The functions chosen mirror and extend the functions
specified in Jones and Caldwell (1979), who felt that the ACs charter
should include: an evaluation and overview of internal audit work; an
evaluation of the external auditor; a review and approval of the
external audit plan; review and approval of the key accounting and

132

financial policies; and a review of accounting statements, annual results and the compliance procedures. Table 13 shows the mean, and standard deviation (std dev) of the number of functions within each of the four categories.

Table 13

Number of functions

	Mean	Std dev
External reporting	4.79	1.50
External audit	5.97	1.86
Internal audit	6.36	2.13
Other matters	2.70	1.59
Total	19.82	4.36

The mean of almost 20 functions suggests that a widely varying range of functions are assigned to ACs by the respondent organisations. This is especially true of internal auditing. Almost half the ACs (48%) assigned all eight of the functions related to internal auditors and only five had less than three functions. The large number of internal audit functions in most financial institutions was cited by respondents in discussions with the author, as an indication of the importance of internal audit in maintaining a sound control environment. An indication of this is that, unlike the industrial concerns surveyed, all the financial institutions had an internal audit function. Functions related to external auditors were also widespread with 55% of respondents having six or more of the functions detailed. The pattern for external reporting was more varied. One-third of respondents had four functions but only one had all eight of the functions listed. Surprisingly, there was no link between the extent of external reporting functions assigned to an AC and the type or status of the financial institutions. One clearing bank assigned only two external reporting functions to the AC; while the AC of one foreign subsidiary had six of the external reporting functions. 'Other matters' covered seven examples of the wider functions which may be given to ACs. No respondent reported more than five of the seven listed and 64% had three or less. The wide differences in the functions of ACs are indicated by the range of the total number of functions assigned to ACs, which were from 11 (a third of the 32 listed) to 27 (84% of the 32 listed) and the standard deviation of over four. There was no pattern to explain the number of functions, either in terms of the type or status of financial institution. For example, insurance companies ranged from 15 to 27 functions; clearing banks from 11 to 21 functions; other British banks from 11 to 27 functions; and UK listed companies from 11 to 27 functions.

The importance of functions covered by ACs was measured in two ways. First, by the percentage of respondents reporting each of the functions listed, and second, by a rank. The rank was determined by asking respondents to rank what were considered to be the five most important functions carried out by their organisations' ACs. The ranks were scored from 1 to 5 (most important to least important). The average score for each function was used to create a hierarchy of the functions for the 30 financial institutions completing this section. The rank column in Tables 14 to 17 reflects the importance of each function determined in this fashion.

Table 14

External reporting functions assigned to the AC

External reporting	% of respondents	Rank
Review company accounting principles and practice, and significant changes during the year	97	2
Review audited annual financial statements	94	1
Monitor compliance with statutory and Stock Exchange reporting requirements	76	3
Review interim reports	67	5
Review entire annual report	61	4
Review summary financial reports	43	7
Review circulars issued in respect of takeovers, defence against takeovers and other major non-routine transactions	32	6
Review prior to issue press statements and advertisements relating to financial matters	30	8

There is a clear consistency between the number of ACs with a particular function and the ranking. In the financial institutions surveyed, ACs were almost always responsible for the review of company accounting principles and practice and the review of annual financial statements. Monitoring of compliance with statutory and Stock Exchange reporting requirements was also present among the

135

functions of a significant number of respondents; although in some cases part or all of this responsibility was attached to a separate compliance committee. Obviously, the last three items in Table 14 are less relevant to some of the financial institutions but even so it is apparent that these functions are of lesser importance.

Table 15

External reporting functions assigned to the AC

	% of respondents	Rank
External auditors		
Review their evaluation of the company's internal control systems, recommendations to management and management's response	94	1
Discuss with the auditors their experience and problems in carrying out the audit	94	2
Discuss the meaning and significance of audited figures and notes attached thereto	88	3
Review factors that might impair or be perceived to impair the auditor's independence	82	6
Review proposed audit fees	67	4
Discuss scope and timing of audit work	61	5
Arbitrate disputes between the auditors and management	51	7 =
Nominate the auditors	34	7 =
Approve the auditors	33	7 =

There is a clear agreement on the importance of the various functions as between the incidence of various functions and the ranking. The functions are typically covered in one or more meetings between the AC and the partner/partners responsible for the audit. There is invariably a meeting to review the annual financial statement and the auditor's report. It is uncommon for the AC to review external audit work prior to its commencement. The emphasis on internal control systems reveals the importance of tight controls in a highly computerised financial environment, where the magnitude of fraud or serious error can be significant to an organisation. The power to review audit fees and discuss the scope and timing of audit work is reported by over 60% of respondents. One respondent stated that the AC had only recently acquired these functions and that the two are inextricably linked. The low ranking of the arbitration function reflects either the harmonious state of relationships between auditors and management, or an unwillingness to admit that disputes do arise. Certainly, positive responses often include equivocal statements such as 'probably although not arisen yet' or 'suppose so'. The power to nominate or approve auditors is reserved to the main board in the majority of cases; however, in approximately a third of respondents the AC undertakes this function. Nomination of auditors is usually based on a recommendation to the main board.

Table 16 shows considerable consistency in the functions carried out by ACs. However, there is a difference between the ranking of functions and their occurrence. In particular, 'discussing with the internal auditors their findings and reports' was ranked as most important by the respondents but was only a function in three quarters of the ACs covered; and 'co-ordinating the work of internal and external auditors' was ranked as least important, despite the function being present in 85% of ACs. The former result is expected because a small number of ACs do not meet with the internal auditors and therefore cannot fulfil the function. In the latter case, the function is perceived as an obvious matter to discuss as both partners are present but in essence the

137

Table 16

Internal auditors' functions assigned to the AC

Internal auditors	% of respondents	Rank
Discuss the effectiveness of internal controls	88	3
Discuss the relationship between internal and external auditors and the co-ordination of the audit work	85	8
Review internal audit objectives and plans	85	2
Review organisation of the department, lines of reporting and independence of the internal audit function	79	4
Discuss with the internal auditors their findings and reports	76	1
Ascertain whether proper action has been taken on recommendations	76	5
Discuss with the auditors their experience and problems in carrying out the audit	73	7
Evaluate the adequacy of the resources devoted to internal audit	70	6

function is of minor importance. As with external auditors, there is a strong emphasis on internal controls, with the three top ranked functions all being related to this area. All internal auditors   in financial institutions, with whom discussions were held, stressed that reporting to the AC enhanced their status and helped to avoid their recommendations being ignored. One stated that it also had the advantage of motivating internal auditors to improve the quality of their reports, since it was usual for reports to be read by directors. On the other hand, several respondents mentioned that discussions were in high level terms and involved only a broad review of the results of internal audit work. However, one respondent mentioned that the AC had the function of reviewing with internal auditors the results of fraud investigations.

Only two functions are widespread. The remainder vary from adherence to the corporate code of conduct, which appears in almost half of the ACs, to reviewing compliance with social obligations, which is only reported by one financial institution. The rankings do not agree with the frequency with which ACs are assigned functions; although there is agreement on the functions to be placed in first and last positions. The main contradiction, the function of reviewing significant transactions outside the company's normal business, was deemed important by all the ACs where it was a function, but did not apply to all the respondents. Other functions, which were mentioned by respondents involve: receive and consider a report by the actuaries of the pension fund; review the management provision for bad and with doubtful debts; establish that the Financial Services Act has been complied with; and liaise with the statutory authority. It was anticipated that more additional functions would have been mentioned. For example Peat Marwick McLintock, see Appendix 3, suggest that ACs should consider amongst other matters: profit forecasts and working capital statements; the risk profile of the institution; and arrangements for compliance with capital adequacy rules. The explanation is probably that in many of the respondents there was a separate compliance committee charged with such responsibilities.

Table 17

Functions under the heading of 'other matters' assigned to the AC

	% of respondents	Rank
Other matters		
Enquire into illegal, questionable or unethical activities	73	1
Initiate special projects or investigations on any matter within its terms of reference	70	4 =
Monitor adherence of officials to the corporate code of conduct	49	4 =
Review the adequacy of management information systems	31	5
Review significant transactions outside the company's normal business	25	2
Ensure the board receives reliable and timely management information	18	3
Review the efforts of the company with social obligations to the employees, the community and others	3	6

Factors affecting the effectiveness of ACs

Respondents were asked to indicate the extent to which they agree that certain attributes of AC members are very important using a scale from 1 signifying 'strongly agree' to 5 signifying 'strongly disagree'. Table 18 shows the mean and standard deviation (std dev) of the responses.

Table 18

Opinions on the importance of attributes of AC members in contributing to the success of ACs

---

	Mean	Std dev
Sound judgement	1.15	0.36
Independence from management	1.30	0.59
Full understanding of purposes and responsibilities of the audit committee	1.42	0.61
Enthusiastic chairman	1.49	0.67
Ability to devote the necessary time	1.64	0.78
Variety of backgrounds among the committee members	1.67	0.82
Knowledge of company's business areas	1.70	0.59
Knowledge of finance, accounting and auditing	2.03	0.81

As might be anticipated, given the nature of the statements, there was broad agreement that the attributes were important since all the attributes had a mean below the scale mean of three. In fact, no respondent reported 'strongly disagree' for any attribute and only nine instances of 'disagree somewhat' were reported. Nevertheless, the summarised responses reveal that certain attributes in the list are considered to be more important than others.

Over three-quarters of respondents strongly agree that sound judgement and independence from management are very important in contributing to the success of the AC. In contrast, only 36% and 21% respectively strongly agreed with the importance of knowledge of the company business areas or knowledge of finance, accounting and auditing. An 'other British bank' respondent stated that it was likely that anyone appointed a non-executive member, although not necessarily a specialist in accounting or auditing, would have a wide enough business experience to contribute to AC discussions. A review of disclosure of audit committee membership in the accounts showed that, in general, there was at least one qualified accountant on the AC.

Respondents also suggested that the following attributes were very important:

an ability to distinguish between non-executive and executive responsibilities and fully understand the non-executive nature of the AC role was mentioned by four respondents;

an ability to identify the fundamental issues in accounting, auditing and the control environment was stressed by three respondents; and

a determination to pursue problems to a resolution was cited by three respondents. One of these stated that a key objective of the AC was to ensure that recommendations are implemented in full.

142

Respondents were asked to indicate the extent to which they agreed that various practices are very important in contributing to the success of the AC. Again, a scale from 1 signifying 'strongly agree' to 5 signifying 'strongly disagree' was used. Table 19 shows the mean and standard deviation (std dev) of the responses.

Table 19

Importance of various factors in contributing to the success of ACs

	Mean	Std dev
Availability of relevant information	1.30	0.47
Ready access to external auditors	1.36	0.60
Ready access to internal auditors	1.42	0.71
Provision of an agenda and related material in advance of meetings	1.49	0.71
Prompt answering of queries	1.67	0.65
Careful selection of members	1.67	0.85
Written statement of objectives and responsibilities	1.67	0.96
Prompt notification of problems by management	1.94	0.90
Continuity of membership	2.21	0.70
Independence from the main board	2.55	1.46
Rotation of membership	3.30	0.85

The results show broad agreement with the practices being very important for successful ACs, with all but three practices scoring below two against a scale mean of three. Even the item 'rotation of membership', which is rated lowest has only 42% of respondents disagreeing. In contrast, the first four practices in the Table have over or just below 70% of respondents stating that they strongly agree. Respondents stated that many of the practices were already in place in the organisation. The conflict between the lack of support for both continuity of membership and rotation of membership needs explanation. The lack of importance of rotation of membership is consistent with the earlier finding that appointments to the AC are normally for an indefinite term. However, continuity of membership, although common, is not deemed to be a very important practice. A typical response was that occasional changes in membership were not harmful and may even be desirable but regular changes would prevent expertise being developed and could be disruptive.

Additional practices which were considered very important by respondents include:

> easy access to chairman by Head Office internal auditors;

> monthly and annual written reports from the internal auditors to the AC;

> regular meetings of the external auditors and the AC; and

> regular examination of the requirements of the AC's terms of reference.

A question sought to elicit the opinions of respondents on three statements using the scale from 1 signifying 'strongly agree' to 5 indicating 'strongly disagree'. The mean and standard deviation (std dev) of the responses are contained in Table 20.

144

Table 20

Opinions on key issues

	Mean	Std dev
Companies with a stock exchange quotation should be required by law to have an audit committee	2.34	1.34
The audit committee should be allowed to use internal audit staff to assist the committee members to discharge their responsibilities	2.49	1.46
The audit committee should be allowed to engage outside technical specialists to assist the committee members to discharge their responsibilities	3.46	1.37

The results, with the response mean being close to the scale mean of three, suggest that there is little positive support for the AC having the powers in the statements or being required by law. However the outcomes reveal the breadth of opinion on these contentious issues. Although, the first statement was strongly agreed with by over a third of respondents; almost a quarter disagreed. A reason put forward for disagreeing with a legal requirement for ACs was that an AC needs the full support of the board, which can only be achieved if it is set up voluntarily. It would also be easy to set up an AC to meet legal requirements but not give it the resources to allow it to be effective. The counter argument is that the law requires many things such as the setting up of a registered office, the appointment of external auditors and reporting requirements about which a similar argument could be put forward. The use of internal audit to assist the AC members in discharging their responsibilities was agreed with to some extent by 67% of respondents but the effect was counteracted by 30% disagreeing to some extent. Some respondents stated that this already effectively happened. As one stated, 'the Internal Auditor has a reporting line to the Audit Committee and, therefore, the Audit Committee can request information or investigation'. The opposite pattern emerged against the proposition of allowing ACs to engage outside specialists. A third agreed to an extent but 52% disagreed, with 33% strongly disagreeing.

Disclosure of the information about the AC in the annual report and accounts

Three levels of disclosure about an AC were identified in the questionnaire: existence; objectives and functions; and members. None of the respondents disclosed the objectives and functions of the AC. However, over 60% of financial institutions disclosed the existence of an AC and the members. Table 21 shows the extent of disclosure reported by respondents.

Table 22 illustrates that there is no clear pattern, as regards the type of financial institution, in the level of disclosure. Non-disclosure is highest amongst insurance companies with a third of respondents not disclosing any information about the AC; even one of the clearing banks disclosed nothing. Where information was disclosed building societies were the least likely to give details of the membership of the AC. It was suggested by a building society respondent that this reflects the large boards in building societies, which derive from their friendly society roots.

Table 21

Disclosure of AC in the annual report and accounts

	Number of respondents	% of respondents
The existence of an AC only	6	18
The existence of an AC and the identity of audit committee members	20	61
No disclosure	7	21
	33	100

The disclosure on ACs varied as to the section of the annual report and accounts in which it appeared. Generally it appeared either in a 'Directors' section (for example the National Westminster Bank, S.G. Warburg Group and General Accident) or the Report of the Directors (for example Smith New Court and the Midland Bank); an exception was the TSB Group, which included the information in a Summary Financial Statement. Further, there were three main ways of giving information on membership. The approach adopted by financial institutions like the Midland Bank and the National Westminster Bank was to list the members of the AC. A second technique followed by the Royal Bank of Scotland, S.G. Warburgs and Commercial Union, amongst others, was to indicate AC membership in the biographical details of directors. Finally membership may simply be annotated on a list of directors as with the TSB Group and Kleinwort Benson Group. In the building societies, it was often the practice, as with the Nationwide Anglia and the Woolwich, for the accounts to be signed by a director styled 'chairman of the Audit Committee'.

147

Table 22

Analysis of disclosure by type of financial institution

	Clearing banks	Other British banks	Insurance companies	Building societies
% in each type				
The existence of an AC only	–	2	1	3
The existence of an AC and the identity of audit committee members	6	10	3	1
No disclosure	1	3	2	1
	7	15	6	5

In general, information on the AC in a financial institution was only indirectly available. This reflects a belief amongst respondents that the existence of an AC is judged to be of little importance by shareholders, investors and others. There is also an opinion that if it is logical to disclose the existence of an AC, it is also sensible to disclose the full committee structure of the board and committee membership. The Midland Bank, for example, follows this to an extent by disclosing the members of the 'Remuneration Committee', which advises on directors' pay.

148

Summary of results

The results of the questionnaire show the following:

The number of financial institutions with ACs

Of the 50 financial institutions surveyed, which include clearing banks, other major banks, building societies and insurance companies, 44 responded to the questionnaire. Of these, 80% had an AC, which included amongst its members at least one non-executive independent director. Of respondents with an AC, 55% reported that there are other ACs, usually below three, within the group. In two-thirds of instances, there are links between the main AC and subsidiary ACs usually through cross-membership or the minutes being submitted to the main AC. ACs appear to be a relatively new phenomenon since the majority were established since 1986.

Therefore, ACs are present in most major financial institutions especially the largest banks, building societies and insurance companies. The main group of financial institutions without ACs are subsidiaries of foreign banks. However, in many of these, there are committees, which fulfil the functions of ACs, but do not include non-executive directors.

The motives for having an AC

The strongest motive reported was good corporate practice. Other important motives were: to assist the directors in discharging their statutory responsibilities as regards financial reporting, enhancing the independence of internal and external auditors and improving communications between the board and internal and external auditors.

AC practices and procedures

Two-thirds of respondents had an AC composed solely of non-executive directors. The number of members on an AC varied from two to seven but the norm was three or four members. Typically, appointments were made by the board and were for an indefinite period. There were no bars to membership of the AC apart from being an executive director.

The ACs of respondents meet three to four times a year on a regular basis for a period of around two hours. The total average annual time spent on AC meetings is 7.4 hours. The duties and responsibilities of ACs are usually specified in written terms of reference. Minutes are invariably prepared for distribution to the AC members and the main board.

Functions assigned to ACs

ACs carry out a wide range of functions involving external reporting, external auditors and internal auditors and other matters. On average respondents' ACs performed 20 of the 32 functions listed in the questionnaire under these four categories.

The functions relating to external reporting, which were present in over 75% of respondents were:

(i) review company accounting principles and practice, and significant changes during the year

(ii) review audited annual financial statements

(iii) monitor compliance with statutory and Stock Exchange reporting requirements.

The functions relating to external auditors, which were present in over 75% of respondents were:

(i) review their evaluation of the company's internal control systems, recommendations to management and management's response

(ii) discuss with the auditors their experiences and problems in carrying out the audit

(iii) discuss the meaning and significance of audited figures and notes attached thereto

(iv) review factors that might impair, or be perceived to impair the auditor's independence.

Only a third of respondents reported that the AC nominated or approved the auditors.

The functions relating to internal auditors, which were present in over 75% of respondents were:

(i) discuss the effectiveness of internal controls

(ii) discuss the relationship between internal and external auditors and the co-ordination of their audit work

(iii) review internal audit objectives and plans

(iv) review organisation of the department, lines of reporting and independence of the internal audit function

(v) discuss with the internal auditors their findings and reports

151

(vi) ascertain whether proper action has been taken on recommendations.

Of the functions under the heading 'other matters', none were present in the functions of the ACs of over 75% of respondents and only the following were present in the functions of the ACs of over 50% of respondents:

(i) enquire into illegal, questionable or unethical activities

(ii) initiate special projects or investigations on any matter within its terms of reference

Effectiveness of ACs

The most important attributes which members for a successful AC may possess were judged by the respondents to be:

(i) sound judgement

(ii) independence from management

(iii) full understanding of purposes and responsibilities of the audit committee

(iv) enthusiastic chairman

Interestingly, a knowledge of the company's business areas and a knowledge of finance, accounting and auditing were not deemed by respondents to be important attributes for AC members.

The factors which were considered by respondents to be most important in contributing to the success of ACs, were:

152

(i) availability of relevant information

(ii) ready access to external and internal auditors

(iii) provision of an agenda and related material in advance of meetings

(iv) prompt answering of queries

Little importance was attributed to independence from the main board or rotation of membership.

Respondents showed little enthusiasm for the proposition that ACs should be required by law for companies with a stock exchange quotation and that ACs should be allowed to hire outside technical specialists or use internal audit staff to discharge their activities.

Disclosure of an AC in the annual report and accounts

Over 60% of respondents recorded the existence of an AC and the identity of the AC members. No respondent gave any information on the objectives and functions of the AC; 21% of respondents gave no details about the AC at all. Disclosure was generally either in a 'Directors' section or in the Report of Directors. In general, information on the AC was not prominent and there was a belief that the existence or absence of such a committee was not of prime interest to the users of financial information.

Chapter 7

A Comparison of the Results from Industrial Companies and Financial Institutions

This chapter has two main sections. The first section compares the responses of the industrial companies and financial institutions. The second section records observations on a number of key issues, which were obtained during discussions the researcher had during the course of verifying responses and subsequent enquiries.

Comparison between the findings for financial institutions and industrial companies

The two populations received an identical questionnaire and therefore comparison of the responses will indicate whether there are any significant differences between the two groups in terms of the number of entities with an AC, AC practices and procedures, the functions assigned to ACs and opinions regarding a number of matters relating to ACs.

The numbers of organisations with an AC

Table 1 shows for industrial companies and financial institutions the percentage of respondents with an AC analysed by organisation status.

The results suggest that ACs are more widespread in financial institutions than industrial companies and that this is true for the four different classes of organisation status identified. One possible reason is organisational size. The financial institutions population was only a fifth of the industrial companies population and chose the largest representatives of the four categories identified. However, a more likely reason is that the institutional and regulatory framework surrounding financial institutions encourages the formation of ACs. The majority of respondents and others with whom this was discussed concurred with this view.

Table 1

Percentage of respondents with an AC

Status of respondents	% of replies with an AC		
	Industrial companies	Financial institutions	Overall
UK based listed companies	65	96	69
Foreign subsidiaries	10	44	17
Public sector organisations	86	100	88
Other organisations	14	70	47

The information on the age of ACs also lends credence to this view. Table 2 shows that 62% of the ACs of financial institutions were founded in the five years preceding the questionnaire, whereas only 53% of ACs in industrial companies were formed in the same period. The period coincides with increased regulation for financial institutions through, for example, the Financial Services Act 1986 and the Banking Act 1987.

However, in both sectors, although some respondents have had ACs for a long time, the extensive use of ACs is a relatively new phenomenon.

Table 2

Age of ACs

| | % of respondents | | |
Years	Industrial companies	Financial institutions	Overall
0-2	21	9	18
3-5	32	53	37
6-8	16	6	14
9-11	13	3	11
12-14	10	9	10
15 and over	8	20	10
	100	100	100

There was a clear difference between industrial companies and financial institutions in the incidence of multiple ACs with only 19% of industrial companies having more than one AC in the group compared to 55% for financial institutions. The mean number of other

ACs in the group was three for each sector. Again a possible reason for the difference is size as a third of industrial companies in the Times Top 50 had an AC compared with only 13% amongst the other respondents in this sector.

Table 3

Motives for having an AC

Reasons	Ranking	
	Industrial companies	Financial institutions
good corporate practice	1	1
strengthens the role and effectiveness of non-executive directors	2	5
assists directors in discharging their statutory responsibilities as regards financial reporting	3	2
preserves and enhances the independence of internal auditors	4	3
improves communications between the board and internal auditors	6	4

The motives for having an AC

Table 3 gives a comparison of the ranking[31] of the main four motives for having an AC in the two sectors.

The comparison reveals a broad degree of agreement on the motives for having an AC. Good corporate practice was the dominant rationale in both sectors. The role of the AC in assisting directors in meeting their statutory responsibilities as regards financial reporting was also highly rated. The main differences were the importance given by financial institutions to the interaction between the AC and internal auditors and the high ranking by industrial companies to the effect of ACs on the role of the non-executive director. The former possibly reflects the importance of internal audit in the control environment of banks; while the emphasis on the latter motive derives from the recent growth in the numbers of non-executive directors (see Bank of England: 1983, 1985 and 1988).

There was also broad agreement on the least important motives. The provision of a forum for arbitration between management and auditors, the possibility of legislative pressure, and increasing the confidence of the public and investment analysts in the financial statements were deemed to be the least important motives for having an AC by both industrial companies and financial institutions.

AC practices and procedures

Although, there was some variation in the practices and procedures among the ACs in each of the sectors; there was an overall degree of consensus. In both sectors, the majority of respondents had ACs

---

[31] A ranking based on the mean of a scale ranging from 1 signifying 'strongly agree' to 5 indicating 'strongly disagree'.

comprising only non-executive directors. The percentage was higher for financial institutions at 67% compared with 53% for industrial companies. Perhaps, this finding arises because on average financial institutions have more non-executive directors than industrial companies. The most frequent composition of an AC, in both sectors, was either three or four non-executive members (38% of the industrial company respondents and 42% of financial institution respondents). There was a similar consistency on a number of other AC practices and procedures. In both sectors, it was normal for: members to be elected by the board; members to have an indefinite term of appointment; there to be no bars on a director being a member of the AC, apart from being an executive director; the members and chairman of the AC to be selected by the board; the company secretary to be the AC secretary; the duties and responsibility of the AC to be formalised in written terms of reference and/or board resolutions; and minutes to be taken and widely distributed. The only areas of difference were the number and duration of AC meetings. The ACs of the financial institutions met on average four times a year, whereas the ACs of industrial companies met only three times a year. The most commonly occurring number of AC meetings a year was two for industrial companies and four for financial institutions. However, the difference in average annual duration of meetings was less pronounced at 6.5 hours for industrial companies compared to 7.4 hours for financial institutions. The average duration of regular meetings was broadly similar for both sectors but special meetings were on average longer for industrial companies.

Functions assigned to ACs

The number of functions assigned to ACs based on a list of 32 possible functions were, as is shown in Table 4, broadly similar both with regard to the mean total number of functions and the split into the four categories.

The importance of individual functions assigned to ACs based on the frequency of the reported occurrences of functions, also revealed strong similarities.

For external reporting, both industrial companies and financial institutions reported that a review company accounting principles and practice, and significant changes during the year; and a review of audited annual financial statements were functions assigned to the AC by virtually all respondents. There was also agreement that reviews of circulars issued in respect of takeovers, defence documents and press statements and advertisements relating to financial matters were the external reporting functions least likely to present in ACs.

Table 4

Number of Functions Assigned to ACs

	Industrial companies Mean	Financial institutions Mean
Number of functions		
External reporting	4.99	4.79
External audit	5.92	5.97
Internal audit	6.29	6.36
Other matters	2.42	2.70
Total	18.47	19.82

Industrial companies and financial institutions further agreed that the external audit functions of most ACs included: a discussion with the auditors of their experiences and problems in carrying out the audit; a discussion of the meaning and significance of audited figures and notes attached thereto; a review of their evaluation of the company's internal control systems, recommendations to management and management's response; and a review of factors that might impair, or be perceived to impair the auditor's independence. In both sectors only a minority of respondents stated that their AC either nominated or approved auditors.

Both sectors reported that each of the eight internal audit functions identified were present in over 70% of respondents' organisations and that the most commonly occurring function was a discussion of the effectiveness of internal controls. Otherwise there was little consistency in the ranking based upon the frequency of occurrence, perhaps because all functions were widespread.

Other functions beyond external reporting, external auditing and internal auditing were limited for all respondents. Over 70% of financial institutions reported that the AC enquired into illegal, questionable or unethical activities and could initiate special projects or investigations on any matter within its terms of reference. For industrial companies, although these functions were the most commonly occurring, they were present in only 66% and 53% of companies respectively. Each of the other functions was reported as being present in less than half the respondents' ACs.

Effectiveness of ACs

The questionnaire examined opinions on the importance of various factors in contributing to the success of ACs. There was remarkable consistency in the ranking for both questions. The most important of the attributes of members for a successful AC and their order of

161

importance were deemed by both sectors to be: sound judgement; independence from management; a full understanding of purposes and responsibilities of the audit committee; and an enthusiastic chairman. The least important attributes were again unanimously agreed to be knowledge of the company's business areas and knowledge of finance, accounting and auditing.

Table 5

Opinions on key issues

	Industrial companies Mean	Financial institutions Mean
Companies with a Stock Exchange quotation should be required by law to have an audit committee	2.11	2.34
The audit committee should be allowed to use internal audit staff to assist the committee members to discharge their responsibilities	2.34	2.49
The audit committee should be allowed to engage outside technical specialists to assist the committee members to discharge their responsibilities	2.91	3.46

Similarly, the most important factors in contributing to AC success and their order of importance were agreed by all respondents to be: the availability of relevant information, ready access to internal and external auditors and the provision of an agenda and related material in advance of meetings. There was also complete agreement that the least important features were continuity of membership, independence from the main board and rotation of membership.

As is shown in Table 5 there was broad consensus between industrial companies and financial institutions on the extent of their agreement with the three opinions given in the questionnaire. Although in all cases financial institutions were less favourably disposed to the opinions – marginally so for the first two statements but more so for the third opinion.

Disclosure of the information about the AC in the annual report and accounts

As is shown in Table 6, the levels of disclosure about an AC in the financial statements revealed some differences between the practices of industrial companies and financial institutions. The results show that although industrial companies are less likely to disclose information on their ACs (35% of industrial companies disclose no information on their AC compared with 21% of financial institutions), the level of disclosure from industrial companies, which do disclose, is higher than for financial institutions. Over 90% of industrial companies, which disclose information about their AC, disclose more than its existence compared to only 77% of financial institutions. Further, 18% of industrial companies included information on the objectives and functions of ACs; whereas no financial institutions gave this information.

163

Table 6

Disclosure of AC in the annual report and accounts

	Industrial companies % of respondents disclosing data	Financial institutions % of respondents disclosing data
The existence of an AC only	9	23
The existence of an AC and the identity of audit committee members	73	77
Existence, membership, objectives and functions	18	–
	100	100

Discussions with interested parties

In the course of verifying the questionnaire and investigating ACs, discussions were held between the author and finance directors, company secretaries, heads of internal audit, external audit partners and other parties. Some of the information gathered has been used in the commentary on the questionnaire. The discussions, as well as covering the questionnaire responses, also extended to issues, which do not lend themselves to investigation by questionnaire. Obviously, the comments obtained are not necessarily representative but it is thought that they might provide some insight into these matters.

Enthusiasm for ACs

Two main stances were identified. In the majority of cases companies with an AC were enthusiastic about them. The reasons for forming an AC among companies which had done so in the previous five years were various and included: pressure from new executive directors with experience of ACs in the UK or US; pressure from non-executive directors; evolution of corporate governance systems to cope with the increased emphasis on financial reporting and audit; and the combination of internal factors and external influences. There was considerable interest in how other companies organised their AC and a general willingness to let the role of ACs expand and evolve. The enthusiasm displayed was not based upon quantifiable benefits but reflected the qualitative advantages derived from involving non-executive directors[32] and improvements in the review by the board of financial reporting and auditing matters. Internal auditors were especially appreciative of ACs and would welcome ACs commissioning special projects. However, the main perceived benefits were related to enhancing the status of internal audit within the organisation and protecting the internal audit function against inadequate resourcing. External auditors were also supportive of clients having ACs. The existence of an AC was not perceived by external auditors as affecting their independence, although it was felt that an AC adds external credibility to the independence of the external auditor. ACs also permit the external auditors to have increased contact with the non-executive directors at both a formal and informal level. In a minority of cases a more cynical view of ACs was taken. Proponents suggested that the diverse functions of ACs and the limited time that non-executive directors had to devote to AC affairs severely limits the ability of the AC to provide more than a 'rubber stamp'.

---

[32] One finance director stated that the AC was 'a training ground for non-executive directors'.

Effectiveness of ACs

The effectiveness of ACs depends on their objectives. The scope of objectives discussed varied from wide ranging goals like improved corporate control to more limited goals like improved board scrutiny of the financial statements and accounts. In general it was agreed by companies that ACs were effective in meeting objectives such as creating a defined area of responsibility for non-executive directors; improving communication between the board and directors; and widening the debate about accounting policies, internal controls and the audit. However, little attention was given to wider measures of effectiveness or to the impact of having an AC on the company's credibility among the financial community. The reconciliation of the limited annual meeting time and the wide range of AC functions was generally explained by the ability of the AC to focus on key issues and review the decisions taken. An approach that is in line with the emphasis on sound judgement as the key attribute of an AC member and the lack of emphasis on a knowledge of finance, accounting and auditing. Internal auditors with whom it was discussed agreed that an AC improved the quality of internal audit work and raised their status.

People dependent

Several persons, including external auditors, internal auditors and AC members, indicated that the effectiveness of an AC depended on the personalities of the AC members (a view which was supported by the results of the question on the necessary attributes of AC members for a successful AC). It was observed by an external auditor that changes in the membership of an AC could radically alter its effectiveness and the way the committee operates. It was also suggested that the debate on ACs is inextricably linked with that debate on non-executive directors. ACs require the company to have a sufficient number of non-executive directors with requisite skills, adequate time to devote to AC matters and independence from the executive directors. However

166

according to some commentators,[33] the pool of available non-executive directors is limited. Therefore, it is possible that as more ACs are formed and as the functions assigned to the AC grow, perhaps necessitating an increase in the membership of the AC, companies will find it hard to obtain an AC quorum. It was also suggested by a company that, although the input to AC work by non-executive directors is valuable, there is a danger that non-executive directors will be diverted from their main role of providing an outside viewpoint on board deliberations.

Expectations of ACs

In several cases it was suggested that there is a danger that the expectations of ACs exceed the output. ACs were perceived by the organisation as a useful check and balance in the wider corporate governance system. However, it was felt that some commentators saw ACs as a panacea for the problems caused by overpowerful executive directors and financial scandals from poor control systems. The research, which shows that currently the normal aggregate annual meeting time is well under ten hours, supports the view that expectations must be realistic, as this inevitably reduces the amount of time that can be devoted to detailed points.

Summary

The results from the questionnaire reveal few differences between ACs in industrial companies and financial institutions beyond the fact that the incidence of companies with ACs is higher among financial institutions. Similar AC practices and procedures, functions assigned

---

[33] 'The hapless and the paradox', Financial Times, 19 April 1991, p.30.

to ACs and agreement on the issues suggest that AC development in the UK has followed a common pattern in both sectors.

Chapter 8

Conclusions

Main findings

The research has attempted to gather information about ACs in order that the debate concerning ACs and corporate governance can be properly informed. The principal findings are:

steady growth in the number of organisations that have an AC

Chambers and Snook (1979) and Marrian (1988)[34] both reported that under 20% of UK companies had an ACs but that interest was growing. The current research found that, at the beginning of 1991, two-thirds of the responding major UK listed companies and virtually all responding major UK listed financial institutions had formed an AC. Further, over half the respondents' ACs had been formed in the preceding five years. The dominant motives for the growth in the number of companies with an AC were that ACs represented good corporate practice and that ACs assist directors in discharging their statutory responsibilities as regards financial reporting. Industrial companies also stressed the motive that ACs strengthen the role and effectiveness of non-executive directors. The main reasons for not having an AC were expressed in terms of bureaucracy and a lack of demonstrable economic benefits.

---

[34] In interpreting these results it must be remembered that Marrian (1988) covered the Times 1000.

169

reasonable consistency in the practices and procedures of ACs

The ACs in both the industrial companies and financial institutions largely conform to the following model:

the AC comprises solely non-executive directors with appropriate executive directors and others in attendance as required (usually the finance director from the executive directors and the head of internal audit and audit partner for the 'others');

appointments to the AC are made by the board and are for an indefinite period;

the AC meets three to four times a year for around two hours with a mean aggregate annual meeting time of around seven hours; the AC has written terms of reference approved by the board; and

minutes are taken and circulated to the board and external auditors.

widening scope of ACs

Marrian (1988) found that the functions of ACs invariably included relationships with the external auditors and a review of external audit work. Other functions present in a majority of companies were a review of statutory accounts, 70% of respondents, and involvement with the operation of internal audit, 51% of respondents. The current survey reveals a widely varying range of functions assigned to the AC by organisations. The findings show that virtually all ACs now undertake a review of the audited financial statements and review the company accounting principles and practice. For companies which have an internal audit department, virtually all ACs review its work and functioning. The breadth of functions assigned to the ACs is demonstrated by the number reported as being present in over 70% of respondents with an AC. The functions were:

External reporting
Review company accounting principles and practice, and significant changes during the year

Review audited annual financial statements

Review interim reports

External auditors
Discuss with the auditors their experiences and problems in carrying out the audit

Discuss the meaning and significance of audited figures and notes attached thereto

Review their evaluation of the company's internal control systems, recommendations to management and management's response

Review factors that might impair, or be perceived to impair the auditor's independence

Internal auditors
Discuss the effectiveness of internal controls

Review internal audit objectives and plans

Discuss with the internal auditors their findings and reports

171

Ascertain whether proper action has been taken on recommendations

Evaluate the adequacy of the resources devoted to internal audit

Review organisation of the department, lines of reporting and independence of the internal audit function

Discuss with the auditors their experiences and problems in carrying out the audit

Discuss the relationship between internal and external auditors and the co-ordination of their audit work

The range of functions is extremely wide given the reported mean aggregate annual meeting time. This finding suggests that AC meetings must be well planned and must focus on the key issues.

Factors affecting the effectiveness of ACs

The respondents agreed that the pre-eminent attributes of AC members for successful ACs were personal qualities, like sound judgement and independence from management, and a full understanding of purposes and responsibilities of the AC. The findings are consistent with the need of ACs to cover a considerable amount of ground in a limited period and identify the main risk areas.

The most important factors that contributed to the success of ACs were identified by respondents as the availability of relevant information the provision of an agenda and related material in advance of meetings and ready access to external auditors and internal auditors. Again both factors reflect the need for ACs to be efficient in order to fulfil their functions.

Disclosure

Approximately 70% of respondents disclosed some information about their AC in the annual report and accounts. The commonest form of disclosure, adopted by over 71% of respondents disclosing information on the AC, was to detail the existence of the AC and the identity of AC members. An extension of disclosure to include the objectives and functions of the AC was provided by only 12 companies. The results are consistent with the low importance attributed by companies to increasing the confidence of the public and investment analysts in the credibility and objectivity of financial statements as a motive for forming an AC.

Future research

This research has provided an insight into the spread of ACs and their nature in major UK organisations at the beginning of 1991. The study provides a basis which can be developed in the following ways:

ACs in smaller firms

Research into ACs in the UK listed companies in the Times 251-1000. Various surveys (Bank of England 1988 and Czartoryski 1987) indicate that fewer companies in this range have ACs. The research could compare the procedures, practices and functions of these ACs with those of UK listed companies in the Times top 250 as described in this project.

173

Effectiveness

Discussions with the firms, external auditors and internal auditors revealed a considerable enthusiasm for ACs. It was apparent that the benefits perceived for ACs varied considerably between different companies and between the companies and internal and external auditors. A more scientific approach could be employed to determine how effectiveness could be measured and to compare the perceptions of the four main parties: the non-executive directors on the AC; the finance function of the firm; the external auditors; and the internal auditors.

European dimension

The AC in the UK closely conforms to the North American model. The UK's membership of the European Community might suggest that European approaches to the needs addressed by ACs should be investigated. The alternative structures are not readily apparent in either the draft Fifth Directive or the Eighth Directive. The latest version of the Fifth Directive does not contain any provisions governing the submission of accounts by the management board to the supervisory board, although a revision to include this under Article 48 has been muted.[35] Similarly, the Eighth Directive on the approval of auditors, although requiring external auditors to be independent in accordance with their national laws in Article 24, does not prescribe mechanisms for achieving this. Nevertheless, a study of relationships between the external auditor and the board in other European countries may well be fruitful.

---

[35] Department of Trade and Industry (DTI) (1990), Consultative Document on the Draft European Communities Fifth Directive on the Harmonisation of Company Law in the Community, DTI, January, London.

a comparison of firms that have formed an AC at a point in time with those who have not

The research could explore differences between companies that have formed ACs and those which have not. A scientific approach with a greater number of variables then were used in the studies by Pincus et al (1989) and Bradbury (1990) could be adopted. The results might yield interesting insights into the reasons behind AC formation in the UK.

Future

The ability to gauge any future direction in which ACs might move is difficult at present since the outcome of deliberations by the Cadbury Committee on corporate governance are unknown and a general election is pending. Three main issues remain: (i) whether there will be legislation to enforce ACs; (ii) if AC formation remains voluntary will the number of companies with ACs continue to increase; and (iii) how will the role of ACs evolve.

legislation

The likelihood of legislation in the medium term to enforce ACs will probably be settled by the election since the Labour Party espouse statutory measures to change corporate governance including a requirement for an AC. While, the Conservative Party prefer a voluntary path possibly because there is a commitment to reduce burdens on business and ACs have the flavour of corporate quangos. Nevertheless, the debate continues with Ian Hay Davidson at the 1991 Scottish Institute conference coming out in favour of legislation on ACs on the grounds that they are essential to assist the auditor fulfil his duty to protect the integrity of a company's finan-

175

cial reports.[36] Whereas, the ICAEW (1991) recommends ACs for major concerns but does not call for legislation.

growth in the number of companies with an AC

It is probable that the growth in the number of companies with ACs will continue. The pressures for this are fourfold:

(i) the debate on corporate governance indicates that ACs are best practice and, as more companies explain their corporate governance systems[37] those who do not follow best practices will need to explain themselves[38] to maintain their credibility with the markets.

(ii) the increase in non-executive directors reported by the Bank of England (1988) also brings pressures for companies to create an AC. New non-executive directors may well have favourable experiences of ACs in other companies or be looking for the defined role that an AC provides.

(iii) in some cases, ACs will be seen as being helpful in dealing with additional requirements on companies in terms of financial reporting, improved control systems and the need for effective auditing.

(iv) an effective AC may, in certain circumstances, provide some evidence that the directors acted reasonably and honestly in the event of criminal or civil proceedings under company or

---

[36] 'News - Non-executive directors', Accountancy, October 1991, p. 12.

[37] See for example Grand Metropolitan Plc Annual Report, 1990, p. 8 and p. 15.

[38] See for example Thorn EMI Plc Annual Report, p. 9.

insolvency law. If the UK environment becomes more litigious, this may be a spur to the formation of ACs.

However, there are also factors mitigating against these developments. For example, the chairman of the ISC was reported[39] as saying that the pool of talent was probably not big enough to provide suitable high quality non-executive directors for all UK companies especially as an increasing amount is being expected from them. Ultimately, growth in the number of companies with an AC, in the absence of legislation, will be dependent on the perceived effectiveness of ACs. Certainly a number of the companies without an AC at the survey date were investigating the possibility of forming one. The decision being based, at least partially, on the benefits, which other companies derived from an AC. Generally, other companies were willing to discuss their experiences of ACs with competitors and did not view the information as being commercially sensitive.

Evolving role

The role of ACs has widened considerably over the past few years and it is probable that it will evolve further. The role of ACs might expand to include: a review of the corporate code of ethical conduct and its enforcement; an investigation into significant frauds; a review of the control environment and the adequacy of management information systems; a review of the compliance of the company with social obligations; and a review of the company's ecological audit.[40]

---

[39] 'The hapless and the paradox', Financial Times, 19 April 1991, p. 20.

[40] See for example Lickiss, M. 1991, 'Measuring up to the Environmental Challenge', Accountancy, June, p. 6.

Summary

ACs are firmly established in UK companies. The growth in the number of companies forming ACs indicates that they are useful vehicles for board involvement in the financial reporting and auditing processes. The formation of an AC and its effectiveness will depend not only on the attitudes and interaction of the members, senior management and the auditors, but also on the time available to AC members to fulfil the AC's functions. Such constraints mean that the AC can only make a limited contribution to improving accounting, the control environment and auditing and that it is not a panacea for deficiencies in corporate governance.

Bibliography

Accountants International Study Group (AISG) (1977), 'Audit Committees – Current Practices in Canada, the United Kingdom and the United States', AISG, London.

Allen, M. (ed) (1989), 'The Times 1000: 1989-1990', Times Books, London.

Association of British Insurers (ABI) (1991), 'The Role and Duties of Directors – A Discussion Paper', ABI, London.

Australian Society of Accountants (ASA) (1980), 'Audit Committees: Are They a Necessary, Self-regulating Mechanism', ASA, Sydney.

Bank of England (1983), 'Composition of Company boards in 1982', Bank of England Quarterly Bulletin, Vol. 23, No. 1, pp. 66-68.

Bank of England (1985), 'The Boards of Quoted Companies', Bank of England Quarterly Bulletin, Vol. 25, No. 2, pp. 233-236.

Bank of England (1987), 'The Role of Audit Committees in Banks', London.

Bank of England (1988), 'Composition of Company Boards', Bank of England Quarterly Review, Vol. 28, No. 2, pp. 242-245.

Birkett, B.S. (1980), 'Perceptions of the Role of Corporate Audit Committees', Doctoral Dissertation, Louisiana State University.

179

Birkett, B.S. (1986), 'The Recent History of Corporate Audit Committees', The Accounting Historians Journal, Vol. 13, No. 2, pp. 109-134.

Bradbury, M.E. (1979), 'Audit Committees', The Accountants Journal, Vol. 58, No. 12, pp. 430-431.

Bradbury, M.E. (1990), 'The Incentives for Voluntary Audit Committee Formation', Journal of Accounting and Public Policy, Vol. 9, pp. 19-36.

Buckley, R. (1979), 'Audit Committees, Their Role in UK Companies', ICAEW, London.

Byrd, E.G. (1976), 'The Benefits of Audit Committees– A Practitioner's Viewpoint', The Accountant, 24 March, pp. 47-49.

Campbell, Walter McNeil III (1982), 'An Empirical Examination of the Relationship Between Audit Committees and the Displacement of Accounting Firms', Doctoral Dissertation, North Texas State University.

The Canadian Institute of Chartered Accountants (CICA) (1976), 'Terminology for Accountants', rev. ed, CICA, Toronto.

Canadian Institute of Chartered Accountants (CICA) (1981) 'Audit Committees', CICA, Toronto.

Canadian Institute of Chartered Accountants (CICA) (1988), 'Report of the Commission to Study the Public's Expectation of Audits' (McDonald Commission) CICA, Toronto.

Chambers, A.D. and Snook, A.J. (1979), '1978 Survey of Audit Committees in the United Kingdom: A Summary of Findings', Working Paper No. 10, City University Business School.

Charlton, M.A. (1977), 'Audit Committees– The First Step Toward Resolving Auditors' Problems', Accountants Weekly, 29 October, pp. 12-14.

Confederation of British Industry (CBI) (1977), 'Guidance on Audit Committees', CBI, London.

Consultative Committee of Accountancy Bodies (CCAB), (1977), 'Audit Committees, Their Role in UK Companies', CCAB, London.

Coopers & Lybrand Deloitte (1990), 'Audit Committees: The Next Steps' (2nd ed.) Coopers & Lybrand Deloitte, London.

Corporate Affairs Commission (1979), 'Final Report by the Corporate Affairs Commission into the Affairs of Gollin Holdings Limited and Other Companies', NSW Government Printer, Sydney.

Crawford, J.G. (1987), 'An Empirical Investigation of the Characteristics of Companies with Audit Committees', Doctoral Disertation, The University of Alabama.

Czartoryski, G. (1987), 'How Audit Committees Split UK Finance Directors', The Accountant, March, pp. 24-25.

Dillman, D.A. (1978), 'Mail and Telephone Surveys: The Total Design Method', Wiley, New York.

Eichensher, J.W. and Shields, D. (1985), 'Corporate Director Liability and Monitoring Preferences', Journal of Accounting and Public Policy, Vol. 4, pp. 13-31.

Grinaker, R.L., Finlay, D.R., McMahon, J.T., and Monger, R.F. (1978), 'Effectiveness of Audit Committees', unpublished manuscript.

Hanely, J. (1986), 'Audit Committees– are we any closer', Accountancy, July, pp. 18-19.

Hughes, S.H.S. The Hon., (1969), 'Report of the (Ontario) Royal Commission Appointed to Inquire into the Failure of Atlantic Corporation Limited', Vol. 3, p. 1653.

Institutional Shareholders' Committee (ISC) (1991), 'The Role and Duties of Directors – A Statement of Best Practice', ISC, London.

Institute of Chartered Accountants in England and Wales (ICAEW) (1987), 'Regulation of Auditors: Implementation of the EC eighth Company Law Directive', TR. 650, ICAEW, London.

Institute of Chartered Accountants in England and Wales (ICAEW) (1991), 'Report of the Study Group on the Changing Role of the Non-Executive Director', ICAEW, London.

Jackson-Heard, M.F. (1987), 'The Effect of the Audit Committee and Other Selected Factors on the Perception of Auditors' Independence', Doctoral Dissertation, New York University.

Jenkins, B. (1989), 'Audit Committees: Where Now?', Managerial Auditing Journal, Vol. 4, No. 4, pp. 14-16.

Jones, K.J. and Caldwell, D.R. (1970), 'The Audit Committee and Bank Integrity', The Bankers Magazine, July/August, pp. 85-91.

Jubb, G. (1979), 'Objectives and Advantages of Audit Committees', Accountancy, February, pp. 103-106.
Kalbers, L.P. (1989), 'The Audit Committee: A Power Nexus for Financial Reporting and Corporate Accountability', Doctoral Dissertation, Pennsylvania State University.

Knapp, M.C. (1987), 'An Empirical Study of Audit Committee Support for Auditors Involved in Technical Disputes with Client Managements', The Accounting Review, July, pp. 578-588.

Kunitake, W.K. (1981), 'An Investigation of the Relationship Between Establishment and Existence of Audit Committees and Selection of Auditors', Doctoral Dissertation, University of Kansas.

Lam, W.P., 'Corporate Audit Committees in Ontario, Canada: An Empirical Study,' Doctoral Dissertation, Mitchigan State University, 1974.

Lam, W.P. and Arens, A. (1975), 'Audit Committees in Practice: A Survey', CA Magazine, October, p. 50.

Low, A. (1988), 'Audit Committees in Central Government', Internal Auditing, August, pp. 233-235.

Marrian, I.F.Y. (1988), 'Audit Committees', The Institute of Chartered Accountants of Scotland, Edinburgh.

Mautz, R.K., and Neuman, F.L. (1977), 'Corporate Audit Committees: Policies and Practices', Ernst & Ernst, New York.

Mautz, R.K. and Neuman, F.L. (1979), 'Corporate Audit Committees', University of Illinois, Urbana.

Miller, H.D. (1988), 'Internal Audit's Safety', Directors & Boards, Summer, pp. 30-33.

Mitchell, A. (1991), 'Accountability is the Key', Certified Accountant, October, pp. 12-13.

National Association of Securities Dealers (1987), 'NASD Manual', Commerce Clearing House, Chicago.

Peat Marwick McLintock (1987), 'Audit Committees in the Financial Sector', London.

Peat Marwick McLintock (1987), 'The Audit Committee', London.

Pincus, K., Rusbarsky, M. and Wong, J. (1989), 'Voluntary Formation of Corporate Audit Committees Among NASDAQ Firms', Journal of Accounting and Public Policy, Vol. 8, pp. 239-265.

Promotion of Non-Executive Directors (PRO NED) (1987), 'Code of Recommended Practice for Non-Executive Directors', PRO NED, London.

Reinstein, A. (1980), 'A Conceptual Framework for Audit Committees', Doctoral Dissertation, University of Kentucky.

Robertson, J.C. and Deakin, E.B. (1977), 'Audit Committee Members' Sources of Expertise', unpublished manuscript.

Touche Ross (1988), 'The Evolving Role of the Audit Committee', Toronto.

Treadway Commission (1987), 'Report of the National Commission on Fraudulent Financial Reporting'.

Tricker, R.I. (1978), 'The Independent Director: A Study of Non-Executive Director and the Audit Committee', Tolley, Croydon.

Van Hoek, A. (1988), 'Audit Committees and the Internal Auditor', 2nd European Conference of the Institute of Internal Auditors, Brussels.

Wallace, R.S.O. and Mellor, C.J. (1988), 'Non-response Bias in Mail Accounting Surveys: A Pedagogical Note', British Accounting Review, Vol. 20, pp. 131-139.

Williams, J.D. (1988), 'The Board of Directors' Reliance on the Internal Auditor', Internal Auditor (US), August, pp. 31-35.

Wolnizer, P.W. (1987), 'Auditing as Independent Authentication', Sydney University Press, Sydney.

Woolf, E., (1979), 'Audit Committees: Are the High Hopes Well Founded?', Accountancy, October, p. 73.

Appendix 1

Audit Committee Research Questionnaire

sponsored by

The Auditing Research Foundation

of

The Institute of Chartered Accountants in England and Wales

in conjunction with

The Bank of England.

1 February 1991

General

1.　　　　Does your organisation have an audit committee?

　　　　　　Yes　　　[　]
　　　　　　No　　　[　]

IF YES PLEASE GO TO QUESTION 5 BELOW

2.　　　　Please indicate by circling the appropriate number from the key below, the extent to which you agree that the following reasons account for your organisation not having an audit committee.

　　　　　Key: 1-strongly agree, 2-agree somewhat, 3-undecided, 4-disagree somewhat, 5-strongly disagree.

1.	audit committees create conflict within the organisation	1	2	3	4	5
2.	audit committees are merely additional bureaucracy	1	2	3	4	5
3.	audit committees are a first step to two-tier boards	1	2	3	4	5
4.	the cost of an audit committee outweighs the benefits	1	2	3	4	5
5.	audit committees act as a barrier between the auditor and the main board	1	2	3	4	5
6.	no legal requirement	1	2	3	4	5
7.	audit committees have no teeth	1	2	3	4	5

PLEASE RETURN THE QUESTIONNAIRE IN THE REPLY PAID ENVELOPE

188

3. Are there any reasons which were not mentioned in question 2? Please specify them below.

    1.   _____ 1 2 3 4 5

    2.   _____ 1 2 3 4 5

    3.   _____ 1 2 3 4 5

    4. Approximately how many shareholders does your company have?

       _____thousand

5. Does your organisation have other audit committees within the group?

    Yes   [   ]
    No   [   ]

IF NO PLEASE GO TO QUESTION 7

6. (a) How many other audit committees exist?   ____

    (b) Where in the group are the other audit committees?   ____

    _____

    _____

    (c) How are the group's audit committees inter-related?

    _____

    _____

7. Please indicate by circling the appropriate number from the key below, the extent to which you agree that the following reflect the motives for having an audit committee in your organisation.

    Key: 1-strongly agree, 2-agree somewhat, 3-undecided, 4-disagree somewhat, 5-strongly disagree.

189

1.	good corporate practice	1	2	3	4	5
2.	possibility of legislative pressure	1	2	3	4	5
3.	assists directors in discharging their statuary responsibilities as regards financial reporting	1	2	3	4	5
4.	strengthens the role and effectiveness of non-executive directors	1	2	3	4	5
5.	assists management to discharge its responsibilities for the prevention of fraud, other irregularities and errors	1	2	3	4	5
6.	preserves and enhances the independence of external auditors	1	2	3	4	5
7.	preserves and enhances the independence of internal auditors	1	2	3	4	5
8.	improve communications between the board and external auditors	1	2	3	4	5
9.	improves communications between the board and internal auditors	1	2	3	4	5
10.	provides a forum for arbitration between management and auditors	1	2	3	4	5
11.	increases the confidence of the public in the credibility and objectivity of financial statements	1	2	3	4	5
12.	increases the confidence of investment analysis in the credibility and objectivity of financial statements	1	2	3	4	5
13.	assists the auditors in the reporting of serious deficiencies in the control environment or management weaknesses	1	2	3	4	5

9. How many members does the audit committee have?

Number

Executive director members

Non-executive members
Other members (please specify)_____   _____
  Total membership   _____

10.   What are the job titles of the executive directors on the audit committee?

1._____

2._____

3._____

11.   What is the normal term of the appointment of a director to the audit committee?

1. one year   [ ]
2. two year   [ ]
3. three year   [ ]
4. four or five years   [ ]
5. indefinite   [ ]

12.   How are audit committee members selected?

	Executive directors		Non-executive directors	
1. by all the board	Yes	No	Yes	No
2. by the chairman	Yes	No	Yes	No
3. by the finance director	Yes	No	Yes	No
4. by a committee of the board	Yes	No	Yes	No
5. other (please specify)_____	Yes	No	Yes	No

13.   Is a board member debarred from serving on the audit committee by virtue of one or more of the following:

1.   holding a substantial amount of shares or loan stock   Yes   No

2.   holding some shares or loan stock in the company   Yes   No

3.   holding a specific office   Yes   No

4.   being an executive director   Yes   No

5.   a lack of financial, accounting or audit knowledge   Yes   No

6.   other (please specify)_____   Yes No

14.   Are appointments to the audit committee (if <u>not</u> made by the board) ratified by the board?

          Yes   [ ]
          No   [ ]

15.   How is the audit committee chairman selected?

1.   by the audit committee   Yes No

2.   by the board   Yes No

3.   by the non-executive directors   Yes No

4.   chairman of company is ex officio chairman   Yes No

5.   finance director is ex officio chairman   Yes No

6.   other (please specify)_____   Yes No

16.   Who is secretary of the audit committee?

1.   company secretary   Yes No

2.   finance director   Yes No

3.   no secretary   Yes No

4.   other (please specify)_____   Yes No

17.   How many times does the audit committee normally meet in a year?

          Number

Regular meetings   ____
Special meetings   ____
  Total annual meetings

18.   What is the average duration of meetings?

           Regular meetings   ____hours

           Special meetings   ____hours

19.   Are the duties and responsibilities of the audit committee specified in:

1. board resolutions	Yes	No
2. a separate charter	Yes	No
3. written terms of reference	Yes	No
4. an informal agreement	Yes	No
5. other (please specify)_____ Yes		No

20.   Are minutes produced for audit committee meetings?

                  Yes   [   ]

                  No   [   ]

IF NO PLEASE GO TO QUESTION 22 ON PAGE 6

21.   To whom are the minutes distributed?

           1. members of the committee

           2. board members

           3. external auditors

           4. internal auditors

           5. senior management

           6. those in attendance

           7. other (please specify)_____ YES   NO

Functions Assigned to Audit Committees

22.   Which of the following functions are assigned to the audit
committee in your organisation?

External reporting

1.	review audited annual financial statements	Yes	No
2.	review entire annual report	Yes	No
3.	review interim reports	Yes	No

4.	review summary financial reports	Yes No
5.	review company accounting principles and practice, and significant changes during the year	Yes No
6.	monitor compliance with statutory and Stock Exchange reporting requirements	Yes No
7.	review circulars issues in respect of takeovers, defence against takeovers and other major non-routine transactions	Yes No
8.	review prior to issue press statements and advertisements relating to financial matters	Yes No

External auditors

1.	discuss with the auditors their experiences and problems in carrying out the audit	Yes No
2.	discuss the meaning and significance of audited figures and notes attached thereto	Yes No
3.	discuss scope and timing of audit work	Yes No
4.	review their evaluation of the company's internal control systems, recommendations to management and management's response	Yes No
5.	review factors that might impair, or be perceived to impair the auditor's independence	Yes No
6.	review proposed audit fees	Yes No
7.	approve the auditors	Yes No
8.	nominate the auditors	Yes No
9.	arbitrate disputes between the auditors and management	Yes No

24. Please rank what you consider to be the <u>five</u> most important functions carried out by your organisation's audit committee in each of the four categories in question 22 and question 23 (use the item number to identify functions, for example, 2 in the category external reporting is 'review entire annual report' and in the category internal auditors 2 is 'review audit objectives and plans'). Column 1 indicates highest importance and column 5 the lowest importance; if you have identified less than five functions in a category merely rank those you have indicated.

194

	1	2	3	4	5
External Reporting	—	—	—	—	—
External Auditors	—	—	—	—	—
Internal Auditors	—	—	—	—	—
Other Matters	—	—	—	—	—

Effectiveness of Audit Committees

25. Please indicate by circling the appropriate number from the key below, the extent to which you agree that the following attributes of audit committee members are very important in contributing to the success of audit committees.

Key: 1-strongly agree, 2-agree somewhat, 3-undecided, 4-disagree somewhat, 5-strongly disagree.

1.	knowledge of finance, accounting and auditing		1 2 3 4 5
2.	variety of backgrounds among the committee members		1 2 3 4 5
3.	enthusiastic chairman		1 2 3 4 5
4.	knowledge of company's business areas		1 2 3 4 5
5.	ability to devote the necessary time		1 2 3 4 5
6.	sound judgement		1 2 3 4 5
7.	full understanding of purposes and responsibilities of the audit committee		1 2 3 4 5
8.	independence from management		1 2 3 4 5

26. Are there any attributes of committee members which you consider to be important which were not mentioned in question 25? Please specify them below.

1._____ 1   2   3   4   5

2._____ 1   2   3   4   5

3._____ 1   2   3   4   5

27.   Please indicate by circling the appropriate number from the key below, the extent to which you agree that the following practices are very important in contributing to the success of audit committees.

Key: 1-strongly agree, 2-agree somewhat, 3-undecided, 4-disagree somewhat, 5-strongly disagree.

1.	availability of relevant information	1	2	3	4	5
2.	prompt answering of queries	1	2	3	4	5
3.	ready access to external auditors	1	2	3	4	5
4.	ready access to internal auditors	1	2	3	4	5
5.	continuity of membership	1	2	3	4	5
6.	written statement of objectives and responsibilities	1	2	3	4	5
7.	prompt notification of problems by management	1	2	3	4	5
8.	provision of an agenda and related material in advance of meetings	1	2	3	4	5
9.	rotation of membership	1	2	3	4	5
10.	careful selection of members	1	2	3	4	5
11.	independence from main board	1	2	3	4	5

28.   Are there any practices which you consider to be important in contributing to the success of audit committees which were not mentioned in question 27?

Please specify them below.

1._____   1 2 3 4 5

2._____   1 2 3 4 5

3._____   1 2 3 4 5

29.   Indicate by circling the appropriate number from the key below, the extent to which you agree with the following statements.

Key: 1-strongly agree, 2-agree somewhat, 3-undecided, 4-disagree somewhat, 5-strongly disagree.

1. the audit committee should be allowed to engage outside technical specialists to assist the committee members to discharge their responsibilities   1   2   3   4   5

2. the audit committee should be allowed internal audit staff to assist the committee members to discharge their responsibilities   1   2   3   4   5

3. companies with a Stock Exchange quotation should be required by law to have an audit committee   1   2   3   4   5

General

30. In the annual report and accounts is any of the following disclosed:

   1. the existence of an audit committee   Yes   No

   2. objectives and functions of the audit committee   Yes   No

   3. identity of audit committee members   Yes   No

31. For approximately how many years has an audit committee been in existence in your company?

   _____ years

32. Does your company have an internal audit function?

   Yes   [ ]
   No   [ ]

197

33.   Approximately how many shareholders does your company have?

_____ thousand

Completed by: _____

Position held: _____

Company: _____

Thank you for completing the questionnaire. Your contribution to this research is greatly appreciated. An executive summary of the results of the research will be sent to you in due course. If you have had any difficulties in completing the questionnaire; please do not hesitate to contact:

Paul Collier BSc, FCA
Lecturer in Accountancy
Department of Economics
University of Exeter
Amory Building
Rennes Drive
Exeter EX4 4RJ

Telephone number: Direct line 0392-263238

                       Secretary 0392-263201

Covering Letter

Dear Sir/Madam

Research into Audit Committees

Currently there is little evidence available on the extent to which major companies have audit committees, the functions and workings of these committees and their value. The enclosed questionnaire is a key part of a research project, sponsored by the Institute of Chartered Accountants in England and Wales in conjunction with the Bank of England, which aims to address this lack of knowledge.

The questionnaire should be completed by the finance director if the company has no audit committee or where there is an audit committee by the person in the organisation most closely connected with the committee. Pilot testing of the questionnaire suggests that for companies with no audit committee the questionnaire takes under five minutes to complete; while for companies with an audit committee completion of the questionnaire usually requires fifteen to twenty minutes. All participants in the research will be provided with an executive summary of the results.

You may be assured of complete confidentiality as, after coding the responses for computer analysis, all questionnaires will be destroyed.

If you have any difficulties in completing the questionnaire please contact Mr Paul Collier. The telephone number is 0392-263238 (direct line) or 0392-263201 (secretary).

Thank you for the assistance.

Yours faithfully

Appendix 2

Specimen Terms of Reference - Industrial Company

Reproduced with the kind permission of Nuclear Electric plc

Audit Committee Terms of Reference

The Audit Committee Terms of Reference for the Company were approved by the Board at its meeting on 5 April 1990.

Purpose

The Committee, which is a committee of the Board, is responsible for considering the systems and standards of internal control within the Company and in particular internal audit and financial reporting. It will also consider annual and interim financial statements of the Company and such other similar statements as may be appropriate. The Committee has no executive role.

Membership

The committee will comprise the non-executive directors of the Company, one of whom will be appointed by the Board as Chairman. The quorum shall be two members. The Company Secretary or his nominee will be Secretary of the Committee.

Meetings

The Committee will meet at least twice a year and otherwise as the Committee Chairman deems necessary. Where appropriate the Director of Finance and the External and Internal Auditors will be entitled to attend meetings, and to speak. The Chairman of the Committee may invite Executive Directors and Heads of Departments to attend meetings. Agendas and papers for meetings will normally be circulated by the Company Secretary or his nominee at least seven days before the meeting.

Duties

1.   External Auditors:

   (i)   To make recommendations on the appointment and renumeration of the external auditors.

   (ii)   To review the scope of external audit and to satisfy themselves as to its adequacy.

   (iii)   To discuss with the external auditors their annual management letter to be submitted at the conclusion of each audit.

   (iv)   To consider the appropriateness of non-audit services provided by the external auditors.

2.　　　　Annual Accounts and Directors Reports:

 (i)　　　To review the draft accounts before they are finalised and submitted to the Board for approval.

 (ii)　　　To ensure that there is compliance with accounting standards, the Companies Acts 1985 and 1989, and any other relevant legislation.

 (iii)　　To review any half-yearly profit figures.

 (iv)　　To review Directors' business forecasts and reports on financial results, management accounts and other financial management judgements and estimates that have a material impact on the financial statements.

3.　　　　Accounting Policies:

To review accounting policies and to have regard to such representations as may be made by the expert advisers.

4.　　　　Internal Audit:

 (i)　　　To review the scope and performance of internal audit and to satisfy themselves as to its adequacy, paying particular regard to reports issued, resources available, programmes of work and actions on its recommendations.

 (ii)　　　To institute special projects and investigations associated with value for money and other efficiency matters following discussions with the Chairman of the Board or the Chief Executive or the External Auditors.

 (iii)　　To discuss from time to time the relationship of Internal Audit with the External Auditors.

 (iv)　　To consider as appropriate reports from Internal Audit.

5.　　　　Regulatory and Legal Requirements:

To review the arrangements for monitoring compliance with regulatory and legal requirements.

6.　　　　Reports of the Committee:

To report to the board as necessary and to produce annually for submission to the Board a report summarising the activities of the Committee during the preceding financial year.

Appendix 3

Specimen Terms of Reference - Financial Institution

Reproduced with the kind permission of KMPG Peat Marwick - An extract from Peat Marwick McLintock (1987).

These specimen terms of reference are intended for guidance only - in practice, terms will vary with the circumstances of individual business.

The Board hereby resolves to establish a committee of the Board to be known as the Audit Committee.

Membership

A majority of members shall be non-executive directors and a quorum will be two directors of the company, and he shall be appointed by the Board.

Members of the Committee shall be appointed for an initial three-year term of office after which their appointments may be subject to annual rotation such that no more than one-third of the members shall leave the committee pursuant to rotation in any one year.

Secretarial and Meetings

The Company Secretary shall be appointed Secretary of the Committee. The Secretary in conjunction with the Chairman shall draw up an agenda which shall be circulated at least one week prior to each meeting to the members of the Committee and the external auditors.

The finance director, the compliance officer and the external auditors should be given notice of all meetings and shall have the right to attend and speak at any meeting. The Committee may ask the finance director and/or the compliance officer and/or the external auditors to withdraw from their meetings.

Meetings will be held at least twice a year.

One meeting will be held immediately prior to the submission of the financial statements to the Board for approval.

Responsibilities

The Audit Committee shall consider any matters relating to the financial affairs of the Company and its subsidiary companies and to the group's internal and external audit arrangements and regulatory compliance arrangements that it determines to be desirable.

The duties of the Audit Committee are as follows:

- to review the annual financial statements and interim and preliminary announcements before their submission to the Board for approval;

- to review any profit forecasts or working capital statements published in any bid document or listing particulars;

- to consider the risk profile of the group and, in particular, to review credit risk matters;

- to review management's procedures to monitor the effectiveness of the systems of accounting and internal control;

- to review arrangements established by management for compliance with regulatory and financial reporting requirements;

- to review risk management aspects of new products having especial regard to control procedures;

- to review the relationship with the Bank of England and/or SIB/SROs and/or the Building Societies Commission;

- to make recommendations to the Board concerning the appointment and remuneration of the external auditors, and to consider the scope and planning of the external audit and review the findings of the external auditors;

- to monitor the effectiveness of the internal audit function.

In addition, the Audit Committee shall examine any other matters referred to it by the Board.

The Audit Committee shall have the authority to seek any information it requires from any officer or employee or any of its subsidiary companies and such officers or employees shall be instructed by the board of the company employing them to respond to such enquiries.

The Audit Committee is authorised to take such independent professional advice as it considers necessary.

The Chairman of the Audit Committee shall make a brief report of the findings and recommendations the of the Committee to the Board after each Committee meeting. The minutes of all Committee meetings shall be circulated to members of the Board.

The Chairman shall submit an annual report to the Board summarising the Committee's activities during the year and the related significant results and findings.

The Audit Committee shall have no executive powers with regard to its findings and recommendations.